Manuel d'exercices
to accompany
IDÉE PRINCIPALE–STYLE VARIÉ

Maurice Cagnon
Montclair State College

Lillian Szklarczyk
Montclair State College

D1707891

1817 **HARPER & ROW, PUBLISHERS,** New York
Grand Rapids, Philadelphia, St. Louis, San Francisco,
London, Singapore, Sydney, Tokyo

TO STEVE

TO MAX

Sponsoring Editor: Laura McKenna
Project Editor: Jo-Ann Goldfarb
Text Design: A Good Thing Inc.
Cover Design: Edward Smith Design Inc.
Production Manager: Jeanie Berke
Production Assistant: Beth Maglione
Compositor: TAPSCO, Inc.
Printer and Binder: Malloy Lithographing, Inc.
Cover Printer: Phoenix Color Corp.

Manuel d'exercices
to accompany
IDÉE PRINCIPALE—STYLE VARIÉ

Library of Congress Cataloging in Publication Data

Cagnon, Maurice.
    Manuel d'exercices *to accompany* Idée principale — style varié /
Maurice Cagnon, Lillian Szklarczyk.
      p. cm.
    ISBN 0-06-632099-2
    1. French language—Textbooks for foreign speakers—English.
2. French language—Problems, exercises, etc.   I. Szklarczyk,
Lillian.   II. Title.
PC2129.E5C34   1989
    448.2′421—dc19   88-24468
                                                          CIP

88 89 90 91 9 8 7 6 5 4 3 2 1

Table des matières*

	Assimilation des structures	Exercices de sélection	Exercices de synthèse A	Exercices de synthèse B†
1. LE VERBE *1*				
1. Verbe anglais traduit par un substantif français	*1*			
2. Voix passive	*1*	*22*		
3. Participe passé	*3*	*23*		
4. Participe présent	*4*	*23*		
5. Participe passé actif	*9*	*23*		
6. Rendre en français un verbe + une préposition ou un adverbe	*10*	*24*	*26*	*27, 43, 55, 80, 93, 105, 118, 143, 160, 182*
7. Être	*11*	*25*		
8. Quelques autres verbes plats à remplacer	*16*	*25*		
9. Verbe-appui	*19*			
10. Faire	*20*			
11. Ellipse du verbe	*21*			
12. Verbes faisant d'un sujet anglais un objet français	*22*			

* Numbers in the body of the chart refer to pages, not sections.

† *Exercices de synthèse B* offer a comprehensive review of techniques studied not only in the current chapter but in preceding chapters as well. Thus, the techniques studied in Chapter 1, *Le verbe,* are reviewed in the *Exercices de synthèse B* of Chapter 1 *and of all subsequent chapters;* techniques studied in Chapter 2, *L'adverbe,* are reviewed in the *Exercices de synthèse B* of Chapters 2–10; and so forth.

	Assimilation des structures	Exercices de sélection	Exercices de synthèse A	Exercices de synthèse B
2. L'ADVERBE 29				
13. Adverbe en -ment *remplacé par un complément circonstanciel*	*29*	*39, 40*	*42*	*43, 55, 80 93, 105, 118, 143, 160, 182*
14. *Tournures idiomatiques avec l'infinitif*	*33*	*40*		
15. Adverbe en -ment *remplacé par un adjectif*	*34*	*39, 40, 41*		
16. Très, *etc.* + *adjectif*	*36*	*41*		
17. *Comparaison*	*36*	*42*		
18. *Adverbe anglais* even (very)	*39*	*42*		
3. LE SUBSTANTIF 45				
19. *Substantif anglais singulier / Substantif français pluriel*	*45*	*53*	*54*	*55, 80, 93 105, 118, 143, 160, 182*
20. *Substantif anglais pluriel / Substantif français singulier*	*46*	*53*		
21. *Substantif anglais / Tournure verbale française*	*46*	*53, 54*		
22. *Substantif anglais / Adjectif français*	*47*	*53, 54*		
23. *Sujet-résumé*	*50*	*54*		
24. *Substantifs à éviter*	*50*	*53, 54*		

	Assimilation des structures	Exercices de sélection	Exercices de synthèse A	Exercices de synthèse B
4. L'ADJECTIF 57				
25. *Adjectif traduit par une construction substantive*	*57*	*76*		
26. *Substantif employé comme adjectif en français*	*58*	*76*		
27. *Adjectif anglais / Complément français introduit par une préposition*	*59*	*76*		
28. *Adjectif anglais / Construction verbale française*	*60*	*77*		
29. *Adjectifs négatifs*	*61*	*77*		
30. *Adjectifs rendus par un adverbe*	*63*	*77*	*79*	*80, 93, 105, 118, 143, 160, 182*
31. *Adjectifs composés*	*64*	*77*		
32. *Adjectif possessif anglais / Proposition relative française*	*67*	*78*		
33. *Emplois idiomatiques de l'adjectif possessif*	*68*	*78*		
34. *Emplois divers de l'adjectif démonstratif*	*69*	*78*		
35. *Les adjectifs antéposés*	*71*	*78*		
36. *Les adjectifs postposés*	*71*	*78*		
37. *Les adjectifs à position variable*	*73*	*78*		

	Assimilation des structures	Exercices de sélection	Exercices de synthèse A	Exercices de synthèse B
5. L'ARTICLE 81				
38. *Emploi et omission de l'article devant un substantif en apposition*	*81*	*89, 91*		
39. *Expressions figées*	*82*	*89, 91*		
40. *Article défini anglais / Article indéfini français*	*83*	*90, 91*	*92*	*93, 105, 118, 143, 160, 182*
41. *De ou à liant deux substantifs*	*83*	*90, 91*		
42. *Omission de l'article: autres exemples*	*86*	*90, 91*		
43. *Emploi de l'article: autres exemples*	*87*	*90, 91*		
6. LE PRONOM 95				
44. *Emploi du pronom personnel* en	*95*	*103*		
45. *Pronoms démonstratifs* ceci *et* cela	*96*	*103*		
46. *Moyens de permettre au pronom relatif de suivre immédiatement son antécédent*	*98*	*104*	*104*	*105, 118, 143, 160, 182*
47. *Moyens d'éviter la multiplication de propositions relatives*	*101*	*104*		

	Assimilation des structures	Exercices de sélection	Exercices de synthèse A	Exercices de synthèse B
7. LA PRÉPOSITION *107*				
48. Amplification en français de la simple préposition anglaise	*107*	*116*	*117*	*118, 143, 160, 182*
49. Prépositions: remarques diverses	*110*	*116*		
8. LA CONJONCTION *119*				
50. Propositions subordonnées	*119*	*137, 138, 139, 140*	*142*	*143, 160, 182*
51. Proposition subordonnée complément d'objet direct	*120*	*137*		
52. Proposition temporelle	*122*	*138*		
53. Proposition conditionnelle	*124*	*139*		
54. Proposition concessive	*127*	*139*		
55. Proposition causale	*131*	*140*		
56. Proposition consécutive	*133*	*140*		
57. Conjonctions: remarques diverses	*135*	*139, 141*		
9. L'ORDRE DES MOTS *145*				
58. Position de l'objet	*145*	*157*	*160*	*160, 182*
59. Position de l'adverbe et du complément circonstanciel	*149*	*158*		
60. Inversion	*152*	*159*		

	Assimilation des structures	Exercices de sélection	Exercices de synthèse A	Exercices de synthèse B
10. LA MISE EN RELIEF *163*				
61. Mise en relief du sujet	*163*	*177*		
62. Mise en relief de l'objet direct	*165*	*177*		
63. Mise en relief de l'attribut	*167*	*178*		
64. Mise en relief de l'objet indirect introduit par une préposition	*168*	*178*		
65. Mise en relief du complément circonstanciel (lieu, temps, manière)	*169*	*178*	*180*	*182*
66. Mise en relief de l'adjectif	*171*	*178*		
67. Mise en relief du verbe	*172*	*179*		
68. Mise en relief de l'énoncé affirmatif	*174*	*179*		
69. Le superlatif	*175*	*179*		

PRÉFACE

This *Manuel d'exercices* has been conceived in such a way as to offer both intensive and extensive practice of the principles and structures presented in *Idée principale — style varié*. Each section contains four types of exercises:

- *Assimilation des structures.* These exercises consist of five sentences geared to one specific point in *Idée principale — style varié*. They are arranged according to the order of presentation of sections in that manual, as indicated by the boldfaced code numbers. At the beginning of each exercise, a model sentence, repeated from *Idée principale — style varié,* illustrates and explains, by means of clear, concise diagrams, the structure under study.

- *Exercices de sélection.* These exercises allow the student to choose among the various French structures that translate a particular English structure and to compare and evaluate these alternative possibilities. Exercises often cover more than one section from *Idée principale — style varié,* indicated by the boldfaced code numbers in parentheses. The exercises reinforce an essential premise of this text: the multiplicity and variety of potential stylistic means at one's disposal.

- *Exercices de synthèse A* and *B.* These exercises provide individual sentences (A) and passages (B) that synthesize most aspects of technique and style in a given chapter. The sentences frequently combine a number of structures and permit both student and instructor to monitor the student's grasp of the general principles and the nuanced details discussed in each chapter. The passages constitute the ultimate test of students' mastery of the techniques they have studied, not only in that chapter but in the course up to that point.

For optimum utilization of the *Manuel d'exercices,* student and instructor should refer to the preface of *Idée principale — style varié,* especially the sections titled "To the Student" and "To the Instructor." It is *essential* that individual techniques and illustrative sentences be carefully considered *before* attempting to complete any of the exercises.

Numerous sentences of the exercises contain verbs, expressions, and constructions (*to be, to have,* the passive voice, for example) that *Idée principale — style varié* specifically warns against overusing and for which it offers appropriate alternatives. This is not due to negligence; on the contrary, we have adopted such an approach as a pedagogical device whereby students gradually come to recognize abuse and repetition, and practice avoiding them by means of syntactical and stylistic variations.

Generally speaking, the exercises represent a relatively formal or careful style (*langue soignée*), and it is expected that the student will translate into correspondingly formal French. There are, however, certain exceptions, and these have been marked with an asterisk. After an individual sentence, an asterisk means that a translation into colloquial or informal French (*langue familière*) is recommended. An asterisk at the head of an entire exercise denotes that the structure itself is colloquial and that all the sentences in that exercise should be translated into colloquial French.

The authors wish to express their most sincere gratitude to Marilyn Gaddis Rose for her unflagging support and encouragement over the years; to Jo-Ann Goldfarb, Bruce Emmer, Michael McVicker, and Laura McKenna at Harper & Row for their patience, graciousness, and editorial expertise; to Charles Mathews for endless hours of manuscript help; and to their students for continuing contributions in the texts' developing stages.

M. C.
L. S.

A gratis instructor's packet of sample translations and teaching suggestions is available through the authors upon adoption of the text and workbook. Interested instructors should mail their requests with proof of book order and course title and number to:

Professor Maurice Cagnon
Department of French
Montclair State College
Upper Montclair, NJ 07043

1 | LE VERBE

Assimilation des structures

1 | VERBE ANGLAIS TRADUIT PAR UN SUBSTANTIF FRANÇAIS

A. Traduire le verbe en caractères gras par un substantif français.

---

                      verbe
Modèle: As soon as she **returned** to New York, she was very happy again.

    ● *Dès son **retour** à New York, elle se retrouvait tout heureuse.*
        substantif

---

1. We hope to see him before he **leaves.**

2. It is expensive to **have** things **dry-cleaned.**

3. For her, it is a chore to **prepare** a meal.

4. I'll telephone your friends as soon as I **arrive** in Paris.

5. **Reading** Baudelaire, you grow intoxicated with sounds, colors, odors, and emotions.

2 | VOIX PASSIVE

A. Traduire le verbe passif par un verbe actif.

---

    sujet   +   verbe + agent
    passif   passif
Modèle: Her beauty **was enhanced** by makeup.

                    ● *Les fards **relevaient** sa beauté.*
                        sujet + *verbe* + *objet*
                        actif   *actif*   *direct*

---

1. Her eyes **were concealed** by dark glasses.

2. The sun **is hidden** by gray clouds.

3. The criminals **will be apprehended** by the police.

4. His face **was illuminated** by a sudden smile.

5. The quaint old cottage **was surrounded** by fir trees.

B. Traduire le verbe passif par *on* + verbe actif.

Modèle: $\frac{\text{sujet}}{\text{passif}} + \frac{\text{verbe}}{\text{passif}}$ He **was never heard from again.**

- *On n'a jamais plus entendu de ses nouvelles.*

  $on \ + \ \frac{\text{verbe}}{\text{actif}}$

---

1. She **was welcomed** with open arms.

2. He **was kidnapped, held for ransom,** and subsequently **released.**

3. **Have** you **been informed** of his decision?

4. The winner **will be notified.**

5. French **is spoken** here.

C. Traduire le verbe passif par un verbe pronominal.

Modèle: $\text{sujet} + \frac{\text{verbe}}{\text{passif}}$ Spanish **is spoken** in the United States.

- *L'espagnol se parle aux États-Unis.*

  $\text{sujet} \ + \ \frac{\text{verbe}}{\text{pronominal}}$

---

1. Portuguese **is spoken** in Brazil.

2. Newspapers and magazines **are sold** here.

3. The door **was opened.**

4. His early paintings **were sold** at a good price.

5. They **were married** in church.

D. Traduire le verbe passif par une construction à la voix active, en changeant le verbe.

$$\text{sujet} \ + \ \text{verbe passif}$$

Modèle: She **is considered** a great actress.

- *Elle **passe pour** une grande actrice.*

$$\text{sujet} + \ \text{verbe actif} \quad \text{(changé)}$$

1. He **is thought to be** an excellent driver.

2. She **was seen as** an expert in her field.

3. A shaft of light **was reflected** off the wall.

4. All his illusions **were shattered.**

5. A still, small voice **is heard.**

E. Traduire le verbe passif par un substantif.

$$\text{verbe passif}$$

Modèle: This composition **was written** by him.

- *Cette composition est son œuvre.*

$$\text{substantif}$$

1. **Was** this portrait **painted** by him?

2. Children dislike **being criticized** by their elders.

3. Actors like **being applauded.**

4. Films and slides **were used** to enliven his lecture.

5. We will insist that all medical leaves **be terminated.**

3 | PARTICIPE PASSÉ

A. Traduire le participe passé par une proposition relative à la voix active.

$$\text{participe passé} \ + \ \text{agent}$$

Modèle: The impression **left by this book** is reassuring.

- *L'impression **que provoque ce livre** est rassurante.*

$$que + \ \text{verbe actif} \ + \ \text{sujet (après le verbe)}$$

1. The evil **done by men** lives after them.

2. She was unaware of the emotion **aroused by her words.**

3. He lives in the house **built by his forefathers.**

4. They saw the sailboat **carried by the waves.**

5. This book is about the injustices **perpetrated by mankind** throughout the centuries in the name of God.

B. Traduire en remplaçant *être* par un verbe pronominal, tout en gardant le participe passé.

être + participe
Modèle: The girls **were embarrassed.**

- *Les jeunes filles **se trouvèrent embarrassées.***
  verbe pronominal + participe

---

1. He **is surprised** and **elated.**

2. She **was obliged** to give in.

3. They **were** slightly **bewildered.**

4. She **is delighted** by his audacity.

5. He **was crouched** in the doorway.

4 | PARTICIPE PRÉSENT

A. Traduire le participe présent par un participe passé.

---

participe
présent
Modèle: She is **lying down** on the sofa.

- *Elle est **couchée** sur le divan.*
  participe
  passé

---

1. She was **sitting** on the grass.

2. The children are **sleeping.**

3. **Kneeling** before the altar, she prayed.

4. He ate a breakfast **consisting** of black coffee and croissants.

5. There is a crystal chandelier **hanging** from the ceiling.

B. Traduire le participe présent par une proposition participe en construction absolue (substantif + participe passé).

$$\text{participe} \atop \text{présent} \; + \; \text{substantif}$$

Modèle: She did not move, **fixing her gaze** on the object.

- *Elle ne bougea pas, **le regard fixé** sur l'objet.*

$$\text{substantif} \; + \; {\text{participe} \atop \text{passé}}$$

---

1. **Crossing her arms,** she adamantly refused mercy.

2. **Bowing,** he began to pray.

3. **Clenching his fists,** he advances towards his adversary.

4. "What shall I do?" she asked, **wrinkling her brow.**

5. **Opening her eyes** wide, she stared at his smiling face.

C. Traduire le participe présent par un infinitif.

$${\text{verbe de} \atop \text{perception}} \; + \; {\text{participe} \atop \text{présent}}$$

Modèle: They saw him **working.**

- *Ils l'ont vu **travailler.***

$${\text{verbe de} \atop \text{percep-} \atop \text{tion}} \; + \; \text{infinitif}$$

---

1. I heard you **calling.**

2. She saw him **building** the house.

3. We will watch them **playing** tennis.

4. Do you hear him **singing?**

5. They like to listen to the birds **chirping** at dawn.

D. Traduire le participe présent par une proposition relative qui se rapporte à l'objet.

$${\text{verbe de} \atop \text{perception}} \; + \; {\text{participe} \atop \text{présent}}$$

Modèle: We can see our teacher **writing.**

- *Nous apercevons notre professeur **qui écrit.***

$${\text{verbe de} \atop \text{perception}} \; + \; {\text{proposition} \atop \text{relative}}$$

---

1. I surprised them as they were **opening** a large trunk.

2. They watched the children **playing.**

3. Did you see them **approaching?**

4. He noticed his sister **singing** softly to herself.

5. Listen to that little boy **playing** the violin!

E. Traduire le participe présent par une proposition relative qui se rapporte au sujet.

---

participes présents
Modèle: She is at the window, **looking out** and **throwing** bread crumbs.

   ● *Elle est à la fenêtre **qui regarde, qui jette** des miettes de pain.*
      sujet   propositions relatives

---

1. A man is here, **demanding** to see the lady of the house.

2. The queen was in the parlor, **eating** bread and honey.

3. He was there, **showing off** his knowledge.

4. They are in the garden, **knitting** and **gossiping.**

5. She was behind the door, **listening.**

F. Traduire le participe présent par un participe présent français après le verbe de perception (noter le complément qui suit).

---

participe
présent
Modèle: One could hear the hail **falling** in the forest.

   ● *On entendait la grêle **tombant** dans la forêt.*
     verbe de   +   participe   + complément
     perception   présent

---

1. I watched the children merrily **splashing** about in the mud.

2. The lovers listened to the nightingale's song **floating** softly through the air.

3. The fisherman could see silvery shapes **swirling** lazily beneath the gray waters.

4. In June she hears hundreds of nestlings **chirping** and **twittering** in the trees outside her window.

5. We sensed the spring thaw **caressing** the black trees and **recalling** the dormant earth to life.

G. Traduire le participe présent par une préposition + un substantif.

---

participe
présent

Modèle: Every day they exercised **by swimming** across the lake.

- *Tous les jours, ils s'exerçaient en traversant le lac **à la nage**.*
                                                    préposition + substantif

---

1. Would you like to go **driving?**

2. He went out **walking.**

3. She used to go **horseback riding.**

4. We went **sailing** for hours today.

5. It is possible to save gas **by riding** a bicycle to work.

H. Traduire le participe présent par un substantif.

---

participe
présent

Modèle: **By reading** good books, you enrich your mind.

- ***La lecture** de bons livres enrichit l'esprit.*
  substantif

---

1. **By meditating,** you relax your body and your mind.

2. You can improve your blood circulation **by swimming.**

3. We forget our troubles **by working.**

4. You can conquer fear **by exercising** willpower.

5. **By coughing and sneezing,** we spread contagious diseases.

I. Traduire le participe présent par un mot ou un groupe de mots en apposition.

---

participe
présent

Modèle: **By being a fanatic sportsman,** he runs certain risks.

- ***Sportif passionné,** il court certains risques.*
  mots en apposition

---

1. He has earned the approval of his employers **by being a conscientious worker.**

2. **By behaving as a devoted husband,** he makes his wife very happy.

3. **By being kind and understanding,** she has endeared herself to her colleagues.

4. **By proving to be an iconoclastic thinker,** he attracts a worldwide following.

5. They have become leaders of the community **by acting openhandedly and hospitably.**

J. Traduire le participe présent par *à* + infinitif.

---

participe
présent

Modèle: They will ruin themselves **by spending** all that money.

- *Ils vont se ruiner **à dépenser** tout cet argent.*

  à + infinitif

---

1. They have trouble **hearing** you.

2. There is much joy **in working** at a job you love.

3. She has everything to gain **by persevering.**

4. We spent the whole afternoon **studying.**

5. He is always **following** us wherever we go.

K. Traduire le participe présent d'abord par *à* + infinitif, puis par *en* + participe présent; comparer les deux phrases pour sentir la différence de sens.

We enjoy **studying.**

- *Nous nous amusons **à étudier.***

Modèle:

We enjoy ourselves **while studying.**

- *Nous nous amusons **en étudiant.***

---

1. We succeed in **working.** We succeed **by working.**

2. I have difficulty **studying.** I have difficulty **while studying.**

3. He hesitates in **speaking.** He hesitates **while speaking.**

4. They learn **reading** and **writing.** They learn **by reading** and **writing.**

5. She dreamed of **writing** verse. She dreamed **while writing** verse. (Employer le verbe *songer.*)

L. Traduire en employant le participe présent pour exprimer une action lente, faible ou continue, qui s'oppose souvent à une autre action plus rapide, puissante ou momentanée. Traduire celle-ci par une proposition relative.

---

action lente

Modèle: In cities we can see pedestrians quietly **strolling** and others **hurrying along** in the crowd.

- *Nous pouvons observer dans les villes des piétons **déambulant** (tranquillement) et d'autres **qui se précipitent** dans la foule.*

---

1. Standing on the library steps, I watched a group of laughing coeds **sauntering by,** jostled by others **rushing** frantically to their next class.

2. In the village street some bicycles **rolling along** were suddenly scattered by a small red convertible **speeding by.**

3. In the swimming pool I saw three white-haired ladies **paddling along** and one muscular teenager **churning up** the water.

4. On the beach we can see bathers **tanning** themselves in the sun and children **darting** around them, **tossing** brightly colored balls.

5. The young lovers **embracing** on the lawn heard voices **shouting,** "Hurray for love!"

5 | PARTICIPE PASSÉ ACTIF

A. Traduire le participe passé actif par le participe passé d'un verbe employé comme adjectif.

---

participe passé actif
Modèle: **Having reached** the house, I rested.

- *Rentré à la maison, je me suis reposé.*
  participe passé/adjectif

---

1. **Having left** the theater, she walked to the bus stop.

2. **Having arrived** just before noon, I uttered a sigh of relief.

3. **Having returned** to his father's house, the prodigal son was greeted with joy.

4. **Having cleared** his name, the senator came home in triumph.

5. **Having fallen** into disrepair, the old castle will become a historical monument.

B. Traduire le participe passé actif par un substantif en apposition avec le sujet.

---

participe passé actif
Modèle: This man, **having acted** in the play, has just been interviewed on television.

- *Cet homme, **acteur** dans la pièce, vient d'être interviewé à la télévision.*
  substantif
  en apposition

---

1. Françoise Sagan, **having written** *Bonjour Tristesse,* became a celebrity overnight.

2. My niece, **having given birth** to a baby girl, is determined to breast-feed her child.

3. **Having received** a scholarship from the French government, the novelist will do research at the Sorbonne.

4. **Having specialized** in international marketing, she accepted an important position with a New York bank.

5. My former professor, **having mastered** six languages, expects to enter the diplomatic service.

C. Traduire le participe passé actif et son objet par une proposition participe passive.

| participe passé actif | + | objet |

Modèle: Having finished their examinations, the students leave on vacation.

• *Leurs examens finis,* les étudiants partent en vacances.

| substantif | + | participe passé |
(proposition participe passive)

---

1. **Having played her big scene,** the star exits.

2. The knight, **having slain the dragon,** released the damsel.

3. **Having published his work,** the great scholar retired.

4. **Having completed her thesis,** the instructor will apply for a promotion.

5. **Having waxed the floor,** the cleaning woman leaves.

---

6 | RENDRE EN FRANÇAIS UN VERBE + UNE PRÉPOSITION OU UN ADVERBE

A. Traduire un verbe + préposition (ou verbe + adverbe) par un simple verbe français.

---

verbe + adverbe
Modèle: He walked out.

• *Il est sorti.*
verbe

---

1. As soon as he **came in,** he **climbed up** the stairs.

2. I'm **going away;** will you **come with** me?

3. Don't **take out** the empty bottles!

4. She **turned around** to **look at** the children playing.

5. They **walked** slowly **across** the road.

B. Traduire le verbe + préposition (ou adverbe) d'abord par un simple verbe, puis par un verbe + gérondif ou un complément circonstanciel.

---

verbe + adverbe	verbe + adverbe
Modèle: She **goes out.**	She **runs out.**
• *Elle **sort.***	• *Elle **sort en courant.***
verbe	verbe + gérondif

---

1. He **went away.** He **skipped away.**

2. I **walked across** the street. I **crawled across** the street.

3. They **went down.** They **shuffled down.**

4. She **went up** to her room. She **fled up** to her room.

5. A little bird **flew in.** A little bird **fluttered in.**

C. Traduire le verbe + préposition par un verbe intransitif employé comme verbe transitif.

---

verbe + préposition
Modèle: This child is **shivering with** fever.
• *Cet enfant **grelotte** la fièvre.*
verbe + objet

---

1. They enjoy **talking about** politics.

2. It is absurd to **cry over** lost time.

3. What a romantic girl! She does nothing but **dream of** marriage!

4. All we ever do at those meetings is **talk about** work.

5. She **smelled of** lavender water.

7 | *ÊTRE*

A. Traduire *être* par *demeurer* ou *rester.*

Modèle: The shutters **were** closed.
• *Les volets **restaient** fermés.*

---

1. The window **was** open.

2. The room **is** empty.

3. She **is** sitting near the door.

4. I **was** convinced of his innocence.

5. The doors **will be** bolted all night.

B. Traduire *être* par *se faire, se tenir* ou *se voir.*

Modèle: The children **are** quiet.

- *Les enfants **se tiennent** cois.*

1. It **is getting** late.

2. She **will be** inconspicuous.

3. They **will be** still.

4. He **was** standing up.

5. I **was** in an enviable situation.

C. Traduire *être* par *se trouver.*

Modèle: He **was** in Paris.

- *Il **se trouvait** à Paris.*

1. I **was** in London at the time.

2. The alarm clock **is** on the night table.

3. She **was** in an unusual situation.

4. The Pyrenees **are** between France and Spain.

5. The hero and the villain **were** face to face.

D. Traduire *être* par un verbe intransitif plus pittoresque.

Modèle: Drops of paint **are** on his hand.

- *Sur sa main **coulent** des gouttes de peinture.*

1. Raindrops **are** on her cheeks.

2. There **is** great sadness in the dead woman's family.

3. God **'s** in his heaven.

4. Countless stars **are** in the sky.

5. Everywhere on the boulevards of Paris there **are** tourists, especially in the summer.

E. Traduire *être* par un verbe réfléchi plus précis et expressif.

Modèle: The majestic Laurentians **are** on the other side of the river.
- *De l'autre côté du fleuve **se dressent** les majestueuses Laurentides.*

1. On the other side of the mountain **are** vast cornfields.

2. Thick gray clouds **were** in the pale winter sky.

3. All along the slopes of Provence **are** terraces and gardens.

4. There on the horizon **is** the steeple of Notre-Dame.

5. Below this plateau **are** lush green valleys.

F. Traduire *être* + préposition par un verbe transitif.

être + préposition
Modèle: A temple **is on** the promontory at the harbor's entrance.
- *Un temple **couronne** le promontoire à l'entrée de la baie.*
  verbe transitif

1. Suddenly a throng of noisy children **were in** the kitchen.

2. Bright yellow dandelions **were all over** the lawn.

3. The Sacré-Cœur **is high above** the streets of Montmartre.

4. A dozen enthusiastic listeners **were around** the lecturer.

5. Many friends and relatives **will be with** him at the airport.

G. Remplacer *être* + adjectif par un verbe.

être + adjectif
Modèle: J'*ai été jaloux* des biens de mon voisin.
- *J'**ai jalousé** les biens de mon voisin.*
  verbe

1. Il *était envieux* du bonheur de son ami.

2. Je *suis heureux* de ton succès.

3. Ils *sont désolés* de vous avoir manqué.

4. Elle *est étonnée* de le voir arriver.

5. Nous lui *sommes reconnaissants*.

H. Traduire *être* + adjectif par une épithète détachée ou par un substantif.

être + adjectif

Modèle: She **was gracious** and managed to please everyone.

- *Gracieuse, elle arrivait à plaire à tout le monde.*
  épithète détachée

être + adjectif

Modèle: **Being honest,** he was obliged to tell the truth.

- *Sa probité l'obligeait à dire la vérité.*
  substantif

---

1. He **was intelligent** and always knew how to take a hint.

2. You **are a coward** and inclined to agree with everyone.

3. She **was understanding** and always said the right word.

4. They **are snobbish** and tend to look down on the common people.

5. She **is in love** and blind to the faults of her lover.

*I. Traduire le verbe de perception ou de mouvement par *c'est* (*ce sont*) en mettant le verbe au temps convenable.

---

verbe de perception

Modèle: With the family, **all you hear is** quarrels and reproaches.

- *En famille, c'est à tout moment des querelles et des reproches.*
  c'est

---

1. In the Rhône valley, **all you see is** vineyards and lavender.

2. In the nursery, **all you heard was** coughs and sneezes.

3. You cannot move because papers and books **are scattered** everywhere.

4. After the child's recovery, **one heard** cries of joy and prayers of gratitude.

5. Once our party is in power, a new era of peace and plenty **will begin.**

J. Traduire *there is* (*are, was*) par *il est, il fut.*

Modèle: **There are** truths that are difficult to express.

- *Il est des vérités difficiles à énoncer.*

---

1. **There are** intoxicating fragrances that bewitch the soul.

2. **There was** a time when he trusted me.

3. **There is** no need to confirm her story; her innocence is manifest.

4. **There are** coincidences that are impossible to explain.

5. **Is there** anything as pure, as fragile as this crystal?

K. Traduire les mots en caractères gras par une expression consacrée avec *être*.

Modèle: Now there's an imbecile **if ever there was one.**
- *En voilà un imbécile **si jamais il en fut.***

1. **There is nothing like** running barefoot through freshly cut grass to bring ease and pleasure.

2. That was the most spectacular sunset **that ever was.**

3. Let us hope that mankind will have succeeded in abolishing war **before millennia have passed.**

4. She is an angel **if ever there was one.**

5. **There is nothing quite like** winning a tennis match to raise your spirits.

L. Traduire en omettant *être* après *dont*.

Modèle: My colleague possesses hundreds of books, **many of which are** in Italian.
- *Mon collègue possède des centaines de livres, **dont beaucoup** en italien.*

1. My husband revels in many little idiosyncrasies, **two or three of which are** extremely comical.

2. Israel numbers twelve tribes, **of which two are** lost.

3. They own six automobiles, **one of which is** a Rolls-Royce.

4. He is exhibiting a notable collection of Ming vases, **several of which are** priceless.

5. They raised seven sons, **of whom one was** a doctor, **one** an engineer, and **one** a captain in the navy.

M. Traduire en omettant *être*.

Modèle: People **say that she is** generous toward her mother.
- *On **la dit** généreuse envers sa mère.*

1. She **thought he was very clever.**

2. He **finds that it is expedient** to flatter everyone.

3. I found many photographs, **several of which were torn.**

4. They **know he is honest and scrupulous.**

5. You **seem to be astonished.**

N. Traduire *être* par *avoir* + substantif + adjectif.

$\dfrac{\text{adjectif}}{\text{possessif}}$ + substantif + *être* + adjectif

Modèle: Her face was still tanned.

- *Elle avait encore le visage bronzé.*

sujet + *avoir* + $\dfrac{\text{substantif}}{\text{(objet)}}$ + adjectif

---

1. **Her eyes are** brown.

2. Why **is your face** scratched?

3. **His hair was** red and **his skin was** very fair.

4. **Their behavior was** rather strange.

5. **Her mind is** keen and **her heart is** tender.

---

8 | QUELQUES AUTRES VERBES PLATS À REMPLACER

A. Traduire *avoir* par un verbe plus expressif.

Modèle: Tramps **have** a life of misery.

- *Le clochard **traîne** une vie de misère.*

---

1. Peasants of the Middle Ages **had** a life of privation.

2. On the other hand, the city dweller (*bourgeois*) **had** a life of comparative prosperity and ease.

3. Astronauts **have** exacting and dangerous adventures ahead.

4. My sister **has just had** a beautiful nine-pound baby boy.

5. She **has** the art of living graciously.

B. Traduire les expressions suivantes en utilisant *avoir* au passé composé ou au passé simple.

Modèle: She **took on** a supercilious air.

- *Elle **eut** un air pincé.*

---

1. She **uttered** ecstatic words.

2. Your mother **burst into** tears of joy.

3. I **assumed** a sympathetic air.

4. They **stared** incredulously.

5. We **shivered** with delight.

C. Traduire d'abord par un seul verbe, puis par *faire* + infinitif.

Modèle: I am going to **call** him.

   • *Je vais l'**appeler**. Je vais le **faire venir**.*

   1. He **showed** us priceless antiques.

   2. She **supports** her family.

   3. He **pointed out** several mistakes in the text.

   4. We'd like to **tell** you some wonderful news.

   5. The wind **was blowing.**

D. Remplacer *faire* + complément par un seul verbe.

Modèle: Il lui *fait la bise.*

   • *Il l'**embrasse**.*

   1. Il *fait un sourire.*

   2. Elle avait l'habitude de *faire des ratures.*

   3. Ils ont *fait des courbettes.*

   4. Cet homme *fait* constamment *des gestes et des grimaces.*

   5. Il n'ose pas *faire un mouvement.*

E. Traduire *to become* et *to get* par *se faire.*

Modèle: Good French cuisine **is becoming** rarer and rarer.

   • *La bonne cuisine française **se fait** de plus en plus rare.*

   1. In recent years she **has become** more accommodating.

   2. It **is getting** late.

   3. She **is getting** younger and younger, prettier and prettier.

   4. The more affluent a society **becomes,** the more preoccupied its citizens **become** with material possessions.

   5. As he grew older, he **became** more understanding of human frailty.

F. Traduire *put* non par *mettre* mais par un verbe plus précis et plus fort.

Modèle: The craftsman has just **put** the pottery **into the kiln.**

   • *L'artisan vient d'**enfourner** la poterie.*

1. They **put** their suitcases on the floor.

2. She **put** her head on the young man's shoulder.

3. Please **put** a coin into the slot.

4. She **put** her wedding gown into the closet and never looked at it again.

5. He **puts on** his overcoat and goes out.

G. Remplacer l'expression en italique par un seul verbe.

Modèle: Les convives *se mirent à table.*

- *Les convives **s'attablèrent.***

---

1. Le malade *se mit au lit* pour trois jours.

2. Elle *mettait* ses papiers *en ordre.*

3. Il *met en évidence* sa petite grue devant le monde entier.*

4. Le vieille dévote *se mit à genoux* devant l'autel.

5. *Mettons* ces documents *sous clé* dans le coffre-fort.

H. Remplacer *dire* par un verbe plus expressif.

Modèle: Le personnage *a dit* sa réplique.

- *Le personnage **a récité** sa réplique.*

---

1. « C'est parfait! » *dit*-elle.

2. Tu lui *diras* cette bonne nouvelle.

3. Elle *disait* souvent qu'elle ne regrettait rien.

4. Il *dit* qu'il y avait bien réfléchi, mais qu'il n'était pas d'accord.

5. « Non! » *dit*-il, « c'est absolument impossible! »

I. Traduire *see* non par *voir* mais par un verbe plus expressif.

Modèle: We **see** this work as a great pleasure.

- *Nous **envisageons** ce travail comme un grand plaisir.*

---

1. He stopped to **see** a glorious sunset.

2. She **sees** her beauty as a handicap.

3. We **see** a great deal of merit in him.

4. Most tourists are eager to **see** the sights of San Francisco.

5. I **see** that the grass needs cutting.

9 | VERBE-APPUI

A. Traduire le verbe en caractères gras par *aller* ou *venir* + infinitif.

Modèle: A thin curtain **filters** the lighting in the room.
- *Un léger rideau **vient tamiser** l'éclairage de la pièce.*

Modèle: A cool wind **cleared off** the fog that morning.
- *Un vent frais **allait éclaircir** la brume ce matin-là.*

---

1. A radiant smile **lit up** her face.

2. Celestial visions **comforted** the young priest during his solitary vigil.

3. Several small streams **flow** into the river at the foot of the mountain.

4. The next morning a scorching sun **burned away** the mist.

5. An unexpected event **interrupted** the festivities.

B. Traduire en employant *savoir* dans une question indirecte après les expressions *il s'agit de, il est question de, la question est de.*

Modèle: **The question is** how many guests will be at this evening's dinner.
- ***Il s'agit de savoir** combien d'invités il y aura au dîner de ce soir.*

---

1. **The question is** where they came from and why.

2. **The question is** how much money we will need to make ends meet.

3. **The question is** when the examinations are to take place.

4. **It is a question of** how much collateral security he is in a position to offer.

5. **It is a matter of knowing** what concessions the great powers are prepared to make for the sake of peace.

C. Remplacer la proposition subordonnée par *voir.*

Modèle: Je désirais $\frac{\text{pronom}}{\text{sujet}}$ + verbe conjugué
Je désirais *qu'elle soit* heureuse et prospère.
- *Je désirais **la voir** heureuse et prospère.*
$\frac{\text{pronom}}{\text{objet}}$ + *voir* infinitif

---

1. Nous sommes heureux *qu'ils viennent* nous rendre visite.

2. Nous ne croyons pas *que vous arriviez* plus tôt.

3. Nous regrettons *qu'ils soient* brouillés.

4. Leurs amis voudraient *qu'ils arrivent* à s'entendre.

5. Il aimerait bien *qu'elle soit* partie.

---

10 | *FAIRE*

A. Remplacer le verbe en italique par *faire.*

Modèle: Le policier observait le voleur comme un chat *observe* un oiseau.
- *Le policier observait le voleur comme un chat **fait** pour un oiseau.*

1. Elle parle à ses plantes comme on *parle* à des enfants.

2. On ne peut pas discuter avec un enfant comme on *discute* avec un adulte.

3. Est-ce qu'ils respectent une femme ainsi qu'ils *respectent* un homme?

4. Elle apprend moins rapidement qu'elle *apprenait* il y a vingt ans.

5. Il choyait ses enfants comme son père l'*avait choyé.*

B. Traduire le verbe en caractères gras par *faire.*

Modèle: She disappeared for a week, as most students **do** at examination time.
- *Elle a disparu pendant une semaine ainsi que le **font** la plupart des étudiants au moment des examens.*   pas de préposition

Modèle: I treat my parents in the same way as they **did** their own.
- *Je traite mes parents de la même façon qu'ils l'**ont fait** à l'égard des leurs.*   préposition

Sans complément après *faire* dans la phrase française:

1. No one will ever love you the way you **do.**

2. She admires dancers the way other ballerinas **do.**

3. Don't do the dishes, I **will.**

4. I will try to perform the task as well as she **would** if she were here.

5. He did his duty as his father and grandfather **had done** before him.

Avec complément après *faire* dans la phrase française:

1. You can't admire a coward as you **do** a hero.

2. One cannot spank an adult as one **does** a child.

3. She calculates her actions as a watch **does** time.

4. You can never possess a human being as you **do** an object.

5. Our employers treat female employees just as they **do** males.

11 | ELLIPSE DU VERBE

A. Traduire en omettant le verbe en caractères gras.

Modèle: While they ranted and raved, **I remained calm.**
- *Eux râlaient, ils braillaient, et **moi imperturbable.***

1. **Nothing is cozier** than a candlelight dinner for two.

2. As far as the eye can see, **there were flat brown prairies.**

3. **It will be impossible to discover** how the prisoner escaped.

4. **The definitive critical appraisal is** that his poetry exudes eroticism.

5. This election will be extremely close; **there is no real way of predicting** the outcome.

B. Traduire en omettant le verbe *can*.

Modèle: From my chalet in the mountains you **can see** Lake Lugano in the distance.
- *De mon chalet dans la montagne, vous **apercevez** au loin le lac de Lugano.*

1. You **can imagine** how happy she is to learn that he is out of danger.

2. One **can never know** whether a candidate will keep his promises.

3. You **can tell** that he is well educated.

4. I **can see** that the jury believes that she is innocent.

5. Many people **cannot endure** the noise of the big city.

12 | VERBES FAISANT D'UN SUJET ANGLAIS UN OBJET FRANÇAIS

A. Traduire en transformant le sujet anglais en complément.

---

sujet + verbe + complément

Modèle: **Drops** of water flowed along the stream.

- *Le ruisseau roulait des* **gouttes** *d'eau.*
  sujet + verbe + complément

---

1. Lovely **flower beds** were scattered throughout the park.

2. The bare **branches** of the trees stood out against the gray sky.

3. The **skyscrapers** of New York rise up into the clouds.

4. The **rooftops** of Paris were silhouetted against the starry night.

5. **Rain** quickly seeps into the parched earth.

Exercices de sélection

Pour tous ces exercices, discuter et comparer vos choix.

A. (2) Dans chacune des phrases suivantes, traduire le verbe passif par au moins deux constructions différentes.

Modèle: Spanish **is spoken** in the United States.

- *Aux États-Unis,* **on parle** *espagnol.*
- *L'espagnol* **se parle** *aux États-Unis.*
- *Les habitants des États-Unis* **parlent** *espagnol.*

---

1. Children should **be seen and not heard.**

2. We **were told** that he had been promoted.

3. Her features **were concealed** by a heavy veil.

4. The defendants **were fined and released.**

5. Upon learning how he **had been cured,** he was overjoyed.

6. His eggs must **be boiled** for exactly three minutes.

7. The wine **was chilled** before it was served.

8. Factories **were started** and stores **were opened** in New England.

9. She **has been** so widely **praised** that she is in danger of becoming conceited.

10. Their words and actions **are** often **misunderstood.**

B. (4) Dans chacune des phrases suivantes, traduire le participe présent par au moins deux constructions différentes.

Modèle: They saw him **working.**
- *Ils l'ont vu **travailler.***
- *Ils l'ont vu **qui travaillait.***
- *Ils l'ont vu **travaillant.***
- *Ils ont vu son **travail.***

---

1. Coming into the living room, she found him **sleeping** on the sofa.

2. **Bowing** his head, the suitor awaited his beloved's reply.

3. She keeps coming to his favorite hangouts, **hoping** to get to know him better.

4. We spent the afternoon **sitting** at a sidewalk café, **watching** the passers-by **strolling** down the boulevard.

5. We could see young lovers **sauntering** along casually, holding hands, and bustling tourists **scurrying** around, as if **hoping** to see all of Boston in a single day.

6. Just **watching** him and **listening** to him, you can learn a lot!

7. He overheard her **talking** about him, not **knowing** he was listening.

8. In the summer they enjoy themselves **swimming, sailing,** or **horseback riding.**

9. **By smoking** you endanger your health.

10. Every morning I hear my husband **singing** in the shower—so loudly that I have trouble **sleeping!**

C. (3, 5) Traduire le participe passé passif ou actif par au moins deux constructions différentes.

Modèle: Having finished their examinations, the students leave on vacation.
- *Leurs **examens finis,** les étudiants partent en vacances.*
- *Ayant **fini leurs examens,** les étudiants partent en vacances.*
- *Après **avoir fini leurs examens,** les étudiants partent en vacances.*
- *Après **la fin de leurs examens,** les étudiants partent en vacances.*

Participe passé *passif:*

1. The damage **done** by the vandals was slight.

2. Many technological advances **predicted** by science fiction writers of the 1930s and 1940s have been realized by modern science.

3. She wore a gown **designed** by a leading couturier.

4. 'Tis a tale **told** by an idiot. . . .

5. The reactions **aroused** by this painting are extremely varied.

Participe passé *actif:*

1. **Having captured the city,** William of Orange granted amnesty to the population for the sake of Princess Oriabel.

2. **Having left the house,** he walked slowly to the bus stop.

3. **Having become an authority on fine wines,** he enjoyed showing off his knowledge to all his friends.

4. **Having created the world,** God rested on the seventh day.

5. **Having arrived in Montreal,** she went directly to her hotel.

D. (6)   Traduire le verbe + adverbe ou le verbe + préposition de deux façons différentes.

Modèle: She **ran down** the stairs.
- *Elle **a descendu** l'escalier **en courant.***
- *Elle **a dévalé** l'escalier.*

---

1. He **hung up** his coat.

2. The plane **flew over** Rome.

3. She **knocked over** her glass of wine.

4. I **ran out** of my house.

5. The dog was **limping across** the road.

6. **Running down** the boulevard, he **bumped into** several pedestrians.

7. He **walked out** of the house, promising that he would **come back** soon.

8. The horse **jumped over** the hedge.

9. Paul **turned around** to look behind him.

10. I will **bring back** all the books I borrowed.

E. (7) Traduire *être* par au moins deux expressions différentes.

Modèle: The building's shutters **were** closed.
- *Les volets de l'immeuble **restaient** fermés.*
- *Les volets de l'immeuble **demeuraient** fermés.*
- *Les volets de l'immeuble **se trouvaient** fermés.*

1. She **was** rosy and smiling.

2. Jeanne's hair **was** brown and her eyes **were** hazel flecked with gold.

3. The pills **are** in the medicine cabinet above the sink.

4. Tourists **are** everywhere in the streets of Sydney.

5. We **were** caught in a traffic jam.

6. I **am** delighted by the progress made by my students.

7. She **was** on her knees.

8. A drop of rain **is** on his cheek.

9. Father **is getting** old.

10. He thought he understood women, but he **was** wrong.

F. (8) Traduire le verbe plat par au moins deux expressions différentes.

Modèle: We **see** this work as a great pleasure.
- *Nous **envisageons** ce travail comme un grand plaisir.*
- *Nous **considérons** ce travail comme un grand plaisir.*

1. He **had** an adventurous life.

2. She **has** a fascinating job.

3. He **said** that he would always love her.

4. "Are you absolutely sure?" she **said** softly.

5. She **makes** all her own clothes.

6. My brother **made** this bookcase.

7. Before you dial, you must **put** a coin into the slot.

8. She **put on** her bathrobe and ran to the door.

9. They **look upon** the assignment as a challenge.

10. She **saw** marriage as a threat to her identity.

Exercices de synthèse

A. Sur une feuille séparée, traduire les phrases suivantes en utilisant les techniques suggérées dans le chapitre consacré au verbe.

1. As soon as I reached home, shouting and laughter were heard.
2. The balcony, which is supported by two pillars, is on the north side of the house.
3. Upon sighting the plane circling above the city, I ran downstairs to sound the alarm.
4. Having returned from their honeymoon, the newlyweds were obliged to move in with the bride's family.
5. Thereupon she went straight off to see the doctor; her eyes were red and her nose was stuffed up, but there was no fever.
6. There I was, abandoned on a desert isle, and what was worse, I was condemned to stay on it until the next steamer.
7. These poems will never be forgotten; merely reading them, I feel more alive, more aware.
8. I did not see them come in, but I heard them laughing together as they passed.
9. She spent an hour picking flowers and arranging them in a crystal vase.
10. The doors were wide open, and several idlers were in the corridor.
11. There has been an accident. (*Traduire de plusieurs façons.*)
12. We were told that snow was on the ground; on the trees were thousands of tiny, sparkling ice-diamonds.
13. I like to walk, and I enjoy bicycling too, along where the placid waters of the Blackstone River flow.
14. She deserves the admiration of her friends; she is never blinded by prejudice.
15. He was always pinching my cheeks or patting me on the head.
16. The question is whether she should go on studying; I'd like to see her start working and earning her living.
17. On the French Riviera, a breeze from the desert warms the lovely gardens almost every day; it is a paradise on earth.
18. In the early morning, from this hilltop far above the town, you can discern Mont Blanc, whose glistening peak stands erect against the blue sky.
19. Clinging to the narrow windowsill, I was forced to drop the pane, which broke on the sidewalk below.
20. She is loyal and conscientious, and she has a demanding and lucrative job.
21. He started running down the street, then, stopping suddenly, looked all around the square.
22. The bare branches of the old elm stood out in silhouette against the rosy yellow of the setting sun.
23. Sitting on their mats, crossing their legs, and fastening their gaze on the spectacle before them, they meditated.
24. Walking into the kitchen, he found his hostess preparing breakfast; seeing him, she smiled charmingly.
25. She hurried out, and soon I heard her shouting herself hoarse at the children who were climbing the trees in her backyard.
26. Once upon a time there was a strange dwarf; he was a clever rascal if ever there was one.
27. He is up in the attic, opening trunks and searching in boxes, hoping to find some old costume.
28. There is no threat of violence in the calmness of the workers' strike.
29. I have only three quarters left in my pocket, one of which is for the church collection.
30. My mother has lost twenty-two pounds by dieting and jogging; you can imagine how pleased she is.

B. Sur une feuille séparée, traduire ce passage en tenant compte autant que possible des techniques étudiées jusqu'à présent.

A half-hour before Sonia Marks was due to arrive, all details of the lunch had been taken care of. The chicory-and-mushroom salad was tucked inside the refrigerator beneath the sheet of plastic wrap, the curry soup had been blended and was simmering over a low gas flame, the black bread was cut and arranged attractively (with another sheet of plastic wrap guarding its freshness) on the bread-board between the two places set with bright Danish mats and napkins, and the butter and cheese had been taken out to soften to room temperature. The first bottle of wine, a dependable Soave Bolla, had been uncorked, for quick serving, and then put back in the refrigerator to chill. Jane walked to and fro in the rooms of her duplex, trying to see the rooms as Sonia might see them, trying to read the person who lived in them. Frequently she slipped into the bathroom and checked herself in the medicine-chest mirror. She was nervous because Sonia Marks meant something to her: Jane looked on her as a winner.

Gail Godwin, *The Odd Woman*
(Harmondsworth, England: Penguin, The Contemporary American Fiction Series, 1985), p. 46.

2 | L'ADVERBE

Assimilation des structures

---

13 | ADVERBE EN -*MENT* REMPLACÉ PAR UN COMPLÉMENT CIRCONSTANCIEL

A. Traduire l'adverbe par un complément circonstanciel composé d'une préposition + un substantif abstrait.

---

                        adverbe
Modèle: He speaks **wisely.**

- *Il parle **avec sagesse.***
           préposition + substantif abstrait

---

1. Drive **carefully!**

2. She has mastered the subject **completely.**

3. They met **accidentally.**

4. That is **undoubtedly** true.

5. We walked **silently** side by side.

B. Traduire l'adverbe par un complément composé de *à* ou *en* + adjectif substantivé.

---

                        adverbe
Modèle: You are interpreting it **incorrectly.**
- *Tu l'interprètes **à faux.***
          préposition + adjectif substantivé

---

1. I read that book **from cover to cover** (= completely).

2. Her fingers caressed his face **blindly.**

3. Sometimes he acts **thoughtlessly.**

4. They were married **secretly.**

5. Fifty years ago, women seldom smoked or drank **publicly.**

C. Traduire l'adverbe par un complément composé de *en* + substantif.

---
                               adverbe

Modèle: She always behaves **maturely.**

   • *Elle agit toujours **en adulte.***
                en + substantif

---

1. He has acted **heroically.**

2. This lecturer speaks **pedantically.**

3. He accepts all things **philosophically.**

4. She talks about wines **knowledgeably.**

5. I always try to act **professionally.**

D. Remplacer le simple adverbe par une tournure composée d'une préposition + un substantif.

---
                 adverbe

Modèle: *Heureusement,* un taxi vint à passer.

   • ***Par bonheur,** un taxi vint à passer.*
    préposition + substantif

---

1. *Apparemment,* il fait cela *négligemment.*

2. Elle est *incontestablement* la romancière la plus originale de notre génération.

3. Nous te rendrons ce service *conditionnellement.*

4. J'aimerais vous parler *fraternellement.*

5. *Enfin,* il a exhorté ses auditeurs à voter pour lui.

E. Traduire l'adverbe par un complément composé d'une préposition + un infinitif.

---
                 adverbe

Modèle: She faced the truth **unflinchingly.**

   • *Elle a fait face à la vérité **sans broncher.***
          préposition + infinitif

---

1. I answered the question **unhesitatingly.**

2. He said that **jokingly.**

3. She irons his shirts **uncomplainingly.**

4. Tell me **truthfully** what you think.

5. **Actually,** we didn't know what to do.

F. Traduire l'adverbe en *-ingly* par le gérondif (*en* + participe présent).

---

adverbe
Modèle: "Bravo!" he said **admiringly.**

• ≪ *Bravo!* ≫ *dit-il en l'admirant.*
gérondif

---

1. "Will you listen to me?" he asked **cajolingly.**

2. "Never mind!" I answered **consolingly.**

3. "Stop that!" she uttered **protestingly.**

4. "You wouldn't dare!" he said **teasingly.**

5. "Trust me," she murmured **imploringly.**

G. Traduire l'adverbe en *-ingly* ou *-fully* par une des expressions suivantes + un adjectif: *d'un air, d'une façon* (*manière*), *d'un ton, sur un ton, d'une voix.*

---

adverbe
Modèle: He studied the painting **thoughtfully.**

• *Il contempla la peinture d'un air méditatif.*
expression + adjectif

---

1. She looked at him **affectionately.**

2. "That's wonderful!" she cried **delightedly.**

3. They have behaved **impeccably.**

4. "Are you coming back?" she whispered **passionately.**

5. "Soon," he replied **tranquilly.**

H. Traduire non par l'adverbe en *-ment,* mais par une expression composée d'une préposition + le substantif *pas.*

Modèle: He ran away **swiftly.**

• *Il s'éloigna à pas rapides.*

---

1. Half asleep, he walked **unsteadily** toward the door.

2. The young lovers walked **slowly** arm in arm.

3. The blind man crossed the street **haltingly.**

4. She scurried off **abruptly.**

5. The storm advanced **steadfastly** behind him.

I. Traduire l'adverbe par un verbe à sens correspondant et rendre le verbe original par un infinitif lié au nouveau verbe.

---

adverbe + verbe original

Modèle: First I **wrote.**

- *J'ai commencé par écrire.*

  verbe   infinitif
  (sens de   +   (sens du verbe
  l'adverbe)   original)

---

1. **Finally** he **understood.**

2. **At first** she **hesitated,** but **ultimately** she **made up her mind.**

3. I **will certainly give** him your message.

4. They **have just left.**

5. We **will probably make** mistakes, but we **will succeed in the end.**

J. Traduire l'adverbe par une proposition.

---

adverbe

Modèle: She is **probably** coming.

- *Il se peut qu'elle vienne.*

  proposition

---

1. **Possibly** he is mistaken.

2. **Of course** he is right!

3. **Nonetheless,** we will leave tomorrow.

4. **Evidently** she is in love with him.

5. I don't know, and **moreover,** I don't care!

K. Traduire en employant l'expression *tant soit peu.*

Modèle: The project appears to me **rather** questionable.

- *Le projet me paraît **tant soit peu** suspect.*

---

1. After several glasses of wine, his speech became **a little** slurred.

2. They arrived **on the late side.**

3. I feel **somewhat** reassured.

4. Please move **a tad** to the right.

5. He seemed **a bit** astonished.

L. Traduire l'adverbe de mouvement progressif ou continu par *aller* + un participe présent ou un gérondif.

---

adverbe + verbe
Modèle: The mist **slowly dissipates** at dawn.

● *La brume **va s'évaporant** à l'aube.*

aller + participe présent

---

1. Dusk **slowly falls over** the quiet garden.

2. That young man is **always chasing** rainbows.

3. The rowboat kept **drifting gradually** farther and farther away from the dock.

4. Her health is **growing progressively** better.

5. Past the top of the hill, the ground **slopes gradually** downward.

14 | TOURNURES IDIOMATIQUES AVEC L'INFINITIF

Traduire l'adverbe par une tournure idiomatique.

---

adverbe
Modèle: **Still,** the family situation troubled him.

● *La situation familiale **ne laissait pas de** le troubler.*
tournure idiomatique + infinitif

---

1. Although they were totally different, **still** they remained good friends.

2. **Surely** you know that good jobs are hard to find.

3. Even though I was expecting it, I was **nevertheless** delighted by the news.

4. After such abundant and widespread praise, she is **naturally** somewhat elated.

5. He is **not any less** dogmatic for being obviously in the wrong.

15 | ADVERBE EN -*MENT* REMPLACÉ PAR UN ADJECTIF

A. Traduire l'adverbe par l'adjectif correspondant.

---

adverbe
(modifiant le
verbe
rose)

Modèle: The mountain rose **splendidly.**

- *La montagne s'élevait, **splendide.***

adjectif
(modifiant
le substantif
montagne)

---

1. She is advancing **majestically** through the crowd.

2. The tiny village lay **placidly** in the shadow of the mountain.

3. "Darling," she whispered **caressingly.**

4. The tower rises **imposingly** above the rooftops.

5. The melody drifts **sweetly** and **poignantly** through the room.

B. Traduire l'adverbe par un adjectif et le verbe par un substantif.

---

verbe + adverbe

Modèle: He **spoke vociferously.**

- *Il proféra des **paroles braillardes.***

substantif + adjectif

---

1. She has **acted heroically.**

2. He **kissed** her **slowly** and **tenderly.**

3. You have **succeeded remarkably.**

4. She **looked** at him **admiringly.**

5. We **congratulate** you **sincerely.**

C. Traduire l'adverbe par un adjectif et l'adjectif par *d'un* + un substantif.

---

adverbe + adjectif

Modèle: He is a **prodigiously talented** musician.

- *C'est un musicien **d'un talent prodigieux.***

d'un + substantif + adjectif

---

1. She is an **extraordinarily intelligent** person.

2. His parents are **remarkably indulgent.**

3. He is an **incredibly generous** man.

4. They are **exceptionally sensitive** to criticism.

5. Have you ever seen such a **radiantly blue** sky?

D. Traduire le verbe + adverbe par un autre verbe + substantif (tiré du premier verbe) + adjectif (tiré de l'adverbe).

---

                       verbe + adverbe
Modèle: You **will succeed brilliantly.**

   ● *Vous **remporterez un succès brillant.***
      autre
      verbe + substantif + adjectif

---

1. She always **works conscientiously.**

2. He **loves** her **tenderly.**

3. They **spoke** to each other **affectionately.**

4. He **laughed triumphantly.**

5. She **caressed** him **lovingly.**

E. Traduire l'adverbe par un adjectif suivi de *à* + infinitif.

---

                     verbe + adverbe
Modèle: They are children who **react quickly.**

   ● *Ce sont des enfants **vifs à réagir.***
           adjectif + *à* + infinitif

---

1. He is a man who **acts promptly** in a crisis.

2. She is not a woman who **frightens easily.**

3. He is a sleeper who **awakens reluctantly.**

4. They are leaders who **move slowly.**

5. That is a scene that **plays magnificently.**

16 | *TRÈS,* ETC. + ADJECTIF

Éviter l'adverbe *très* (*fort, bien, extrêmement,* etc.) par l'emploi d'un adjectif plus précis, plus imagé.

---

                        très + adjectif
Modèle: He is a **very enthusiastic** musicologist.

    ● *C'est un musicologue **passionné.***
                        adjectif plus puissant

---

1. She is a **very close** friend.

2. That was a **very grand** sight.

3. The sequoia is a **very tall** tree.

4. She was an **extremely large** woman.

5. He seemed **very happy.**

17 | COMPARAISON

A. Traduire le mot *like* par *tel, tel que* ou *ainsi que.*

Modèle: The stranger, **like** a ghost, directed us toward him.

    ● *L'étranger, **tel** un revenant, nous dirigea vers lui.*

---

1. The house, **like** a museum, was furnished with rare and precious antiques.

2. The stunned winner of the grand prize advanced toward the platform **like** a sleepwalker.

3. She smiled gravely, **like** a medieval madonna.

4. The little boy frolics and gambols in the water, **like** a fish.

5. A large golden moon rolled **like** an orange among the clouds.

B. Traduire le mot *like* par *comme qui dirait,* on dirait (de)* (sens présent) ou *on aurait dit* (sens passé).

Modèle: It is **like** a rainbow and yet there has been no rain.

    ● ***On dirait** un arc-en-ciel et pourtant il n'a pas plu.*

---

1. She moves forward smoothly and silently, **like** a panther.

2. In the branches, bits of ice sparkled in the sun **like** diamonds.

3. His coat is stained with tomato juice, **like** rust.

4. The ballerina whirled round and round, **like** a spinning top.

5. **Like** a hunchback, he walks all bent over.

C. Traduire le mot *as* par *comme* dans les expressions figées.

Modèle: He was as white **as** a sheet.
- *Il était blanc **comme** un linge.*

---

1. He is as brave **as** a lion.

2. It is as hard **as** iron.

3. She is as red **as** a tomato.

4. He was as gentle **as** a lamb.

5. This child is as good **as** gold.

D. Traduire les deux phrases en les comparant, afin de ressentir la valeur atténuante de *comme.*

One felt in him a hint of uneasiness.
- *On ressentait chez lui un soupçon de malaise.*

Modèle:
One felt in him a hint of uneasiness, **as it were.**
- *On ressentait chez lui **comme** un soupçon de malaise.*

---

1. I felt a shiver. I felt **a kind of** shiver.

2. She stood there thunderstruck. She stood there **as if** thunderstruck.

3. He is bewitched. He is **as if** bewitched.

4. I felt compassion. I felt **something akin to** compassion.

5. She was dazzled. She was dazzled, **you might say.**

E. Traduire l'action supposée ou imaginée, dans la proposition relative après *comme,* par un verbe au conditionnel (présent ou passé).

Modèle: The child imagines that the scudding clouds are magical birds **flying off** to faraway islands.
- *L'enfant imagine les nuages mobiles comme des oiseaux magiques **qui s'envoleraient** vers des îles lointaines.*

---

1. The snow was white and soft, like absorbent cotton that **might have spread out** all over the ground.

2. The birch tree stands pale and slender like a bride whose veil **might be woven** out of moonbeams.

3. She appears unbelievably fragile, like a Dresden figurine that **might break** at a touch.

4. To the little boy, the moon seemed very near, rather like a huge croissant that he **might grab** and **gobble up.**

5. She has a fiercely watchful air, like a lioness **guarding** her cubs.

F. Employer *auprès de, à côté de* ou *au prix de* pour traduire *in comparison with, compared to (with).*

Modèle: It is a lot **compared to** what I had hoped for.

- *C'est beaucoup **au prix de** ce que j'avais souhaité.*

1. This is a big city **in comparison with** my little village.

2. Real life is dull **compared to** daydreams.

3. She is a genius **compared with** her brother.

4. This is a banquet **in comparison with** our usual dinners!

5. This is nothing **compared to** what we were expecting.

G. Traduire *much more, far more, considerably more* par l'adverbe *autrement* ou la locution adverbiale *bien autrement* ou *tout autrement.*

Modèle: That problem is **far more** serious.

- *Ce problème-là est **(bien) autrement** sérieux.*

1. She is in love with him **far more** than we had thought.

2. This is a **far braver** act than anything he has ever done before.

3. Our ancestors had **much heartier** appetites than we do.

4. This time, he has achieved a **far more** impressive success.

5. In France, professors are **considerably more** demanding.

H. Traduire en employant *autre* avec une valeur comparative.

Modèle: The ceremony was **altogether more** splendid.

- *La cérémonie fut d'une **tout autre** splendeur.*

1. Ours is a **far greater** happiness.

2. Her eyes are **a lot bluer** and her smile **a lot sweeter.**

3. We then sensed a **much more** intense emotion.

4. What he feels now is a **considerably greater** pride.

5. She was **far more** beautiful.

18 │ ADVERBE ANGLAIS *EVEN* (*VERY*)

A. Traduire *even, very* par *jusqu'à,* devant l'objet direct.

Modèle: I have forgotten his **very** existence on earth.
- *J'ai oublié jusqu'à son existence sur terre.*

1. He teases everyone, **even** his own children.

2. We sold everything, **even** our own books.

3. She would have given her **very** life for his sake.

4. I love all living creatures, **even** mosquitos.

5. He knows our **very** inmost thoughts.

B. Traduire *even, very,* devant le sujet, par *il n'y a pas* (*il n'est pas*) *jusqu'à* + substantif + proposition relative dont le verbe, au subjonctif, est précédé de *ne.*

Modèle: **Even** professors know the answer.
- ***Il n'y a pas jusqu'aux*** *professeurs qui ne sachent la réponse.*

1. **Even** his son pities him.

2. **Even** your enemies respect you.

3. A hush falls over the garden; **even** the birds are silent.

4. In her house, **even** the dishcloths are marked with the fleur-de-lys!

5. In this affluent society, **even** the poorest family can own an automobile.

Exercices de sélection

Pour tous ces exercices, discuter et comparer vos choix.

A. (13, 15) Traduire l'adverbe par au moins deux constructions différentes.

Modèle: "You wouldn't dare!" she says **teasingly**.
- « *Tu n'oserais pas!* » *dit-elle,* ***taquine.***
- « *Tu n'oserais pas!* » *dit-elle* ***sur un ton taquin.***
- « *Tu n'oserais pas!* » *dit-elle* ***d'un air taquin.***
- « *Tu n'oserais pas!* » *dit-elle* ***en le taquinant.***

1. He looked at her **cheerfully.**

2. She spoke **hesitatingly.**

3. They embraced **passionately.**

4. He turns and walks away **resolutely.**

5. You should never take what he says **literally.**

6. **Apparently** nothing has yet been decided.

7. She smiled **enchantingly.**

8. "Don't be selfish!" he said **reproachfully.**

9. They ate their dinner **silently.**

10. This is **undoubtedly** a masterpiece.

B. (13, 14, 15)   Traduire l'adverbe par au moins deux constructions différentes.

Modèle: Surely he knows the risks we are running!

- *Il n'est pas sans* connaître les risques que nous courons!
- *Il connaît à coup sûr* les risques que nous courons!
- *Il connaît sans doute* les risques que nous courons!
- *Il va sans dire qu'*il connaît les risques que nous courons!

---

1. I will **certainly** tell her that you called.

2. She is **probably** coming much later.

3. **Finally** they made up their minds.

4. **Surely** you realize the responsibilities of marriage!

5. She cried out **delightedly.**

6. They chatter **incessantly.**

7. Although he tries to look at things philosophically, little things continue to annoy him **nevertheless.**

8. The serpent spoke to Eve **cajolingly.**

9. **Truthfully,** I think you are mistaken.

10. **Naturally** you understand that this situation cannot go on indefinitely.

C. (15) Traduire l'adverbe encombrant par au moins deux constructions différentes.

Modèle: She was a **radiantly vital** creature.
- *C'était un être **d'une vitalité radieuse**.*
- *C'était un être **rayonnant de vitalité**.*
- *C'était un être **rayonnant, dynamique**.*

1. He is an **admirably patient** man.

2. His daughter is an **incredibly beautiful** young woman.

3. This is an **undeniably significant** contribution.

4. He was an **exceptionally shy** child.

5. She is a **remarkably talented** painter.

6. He stood **contemptuously aloof**.

7. She is reputed to be **outstandingly intelligent**.

8. You are an **amazingly perceptive** listener.

9. We have been **extraordinarily lucky**.

10. This kitchen is **impeccably clean!**

D. (16) Traduire *very* + adjectif par au moins deux constructions différentes.

Modèle: She is **very happy**.
- *Elle est **ravie**.*
- *Elle est **aux anges**.*

1. I am **very sorry** to disappoint you.

2. Odile was **very beautiful**.

3. Quasimodo was **very ugly**.

4. Gigi had a **very small** nose.

5. The captain is a **very tall** man.

6. You are **very sweet**.

7. That's a **very bright** idea.

8. His mother cooked **very good** meals.

9. He got **very fat.**

10. She is a **very charming** woman.

E. (17, 18) Traduire le terme en caractères gras par au moins deux constructions différentes.

Modèle: The lake shimmers in the sunlight **like** a mirror.

- *Le lac, **tel** un miroir, reluit sous le soleil.*
- *Le lac reluit sous le soleil, **ainsi qu'**un miroir.*
- *Le lac reluit sous le soleil; **on dirait** un miroir.*

---

1. Her eyes glowed **like** live coals.

2. The subway stretches out for miles, **like** a vast underground city.

3. I felt **something akin to** a shudder.

4. He devoured his sandwich **like** a hungry wolf.

5. The stars were sparkling **like** jewels against a black velvet background.

6. This house is like a castle **in comparison with** my tiny cottage.

7. The matter is **considerably more** serious than he realizes.

8. He worships the **very** ground she walks on.

9. I packed everything, **even** my toothbrush.

10. In her house **even** the newspapers are antiques!

Exercices de synthèse

A. Sur une feuille séparée, traduire les phrases suivantes en utilisant les techniques suggérées dans le chapitre consacré à l'adverbe.

1. These lessons are getting shorter and shorter all the time, but they are far more difficult than the first ones.
2. Even the pedestrians had trouble in fighting their way through the snowdrifts.
3. The foregoing circumstances had evidently blocked her plans completely.
4. Anyhow, he will probably begin over again very soon.
5. We had unwittingly entered a huge cave; you would have thought it a subterranean ballroom.
6. The document was discovered quite accidentally, but apparently its importance has been constantly increasing.
7. Whenever I see mountains, I invariably feel a touch of homesickness.
8. He is never grouchy or sullen, but cheerful, optimistic, and really very likable.
9. Stealthily, she tiptoed through the apartment; fortunately, she only woke the dog.
10. We passed unthinkingly before the open door. What a racket! Just like an insane asylum.

11. Suddenly they began to laugh uproariously; it was truly a peal of uncontrollable laughter.
12. You will doubtless hear from her soon; her silence is nevertheless just a bit disconcerting at the present time.
13. Night was falling silently, the sky grew darker and darker, and the air was exquisitely fragrant; it was indeed an unimaginably beautiful night.
14. Even the stones of the walls would have cried out, had they had tongues.
15. "Oh yes, you dance charmingly," she called back mockingly.
16. Ordinarily the tiny mountain lake lies quietly, bathed in the brilliantly beautiful moonlight.
17. Moreover, that is my secret; naturally I am not going to tell you what I overheard.
18. "The party has unquestionably chosen the wrong policy," declaimed the speaker pessimistically.
19. He is not actually an author; he has merely written a few essays for locally published newspapers.
20. All this wealth is nothing compared to the happiness that you have actually lost in gaining it.
21. The poor man was extraordinarily awkward, but he won out by persevering patiently.
22. "She is very clever," he continued admiringly, "and moreover, she is far more modest than I expected."
23. He hesitated at first, but he nevertheless acted heroically in the end.
24. One who fails after trying courageously is far more noble than one who is easily successful.
25. Nothing is so ridiculous as a person who hangs around idly in the house day in and day out.
26. Although she belittles her son publicly, she is secretly proud of his talent nonetheless.
27. A large, brightly colored butterfly fluttered lazily above the rosebushes.
28. "You are behaving idiotically!" she says rebukingly; he accepts the reprimand unprotestingly.
29. He gave unstintingly, spent prodigally, and gambled incessantly; finally he lost everything, even his house and furniture.
30. She did not really believe that anything could be suitably organized or carried out without her assistance.

B. Sur une feuille séparée, traduire ce passage en tenant compte autant que possible des techniques étudiées jusqu'à présent.

It is the quality of light I remember most intensely about that morning when it all started to happen, and how Sam's body seems to float in it. The light has simply bleached away all traces of blanket and floor and there she is, buoyed up by layers of fluid light. She appears to be crafted out of the light, so continuously and harmoniously do the parts of her body mesh with its contours. And yet I need her outline, too. Otherwise it will be just blobs of light. The linear plane of her individuality must be there so that the light will have a special form to keep afloat.

She is lying on her back, the solid flank nearest me crossed at the peak of the other upraised knee. Her breasts slope away from each other and the strong, taut arms stretch above her head, obscuring the lower part of her face. She is studying, lying down. It is amazing how long she can keep her arms raised like that, holding the big orange-and-green manual which promises her the rest of her high school education.

I'll leave out the book, I think: just fade out suggestively at the top of the canvas and make it as if her hands are reaching for something they already grasp. The main thing is to get the model sketched in and then, quickly, over the pencil outline, try to capture those fugitive contours of light.

Gail Godwin, *Violet Clay*
(Harmondsworth, England: Penguin, 1986), pp. 306–307.

3 | LE SUBSTANTIF

Assimilation des structures

19 | SUBSTANTIF ANGLAIS SINGULIER / SUBSTANTIF FRANÇAIS PLURIEL

A. Traduire le substantif anglais par un substantif français pluriel.

singulier

Modèle: That is a woman of endless **resource.**

- *C'est là une femme inépuisable en **ressources.***

pluriel

1. She has a good head for **business.**

2. He was proud of his wife's **success.**

3. That task will not pose any **difficulty.**

4. I long to experience the **joy** of family life.

5. We are deeply grateful for the **kindness** you have shown us.

B. Traduire le substantif anglais par un substantif français pluriel.

Modèle: He explored the ocean **deep** in a bathysphere.

- *Il explora **les abîmes** de l'océan dans une bathysphère.*

1. She contemplated for a moment the **sparkle** of the large square diamond.

2. The frigid winter **cold** does not discourage the fanatic sportsman addicted to cross-country skiing.

3. Within five minutes the building was surrounded by firemen and **firefighting equipment.**

4. The balloon rose into the **air.**

5. **Within the space of a single day,** our life had changed radically.

20 | SUBSTANTIF ANGLAIS PLURIEL / SUBSTANTIF FRANÇAIS SINGULIER

A. Traduire le substantif anglais pluriel par un substantif français singulier.

---

pluriel

Modèle: The women took off their **hats** and **coats.**

● *Les dames enlevèrent leur **chapeau** et leur **manteau.***

singulier

---

1. They put on their **raincoats** over their **pajamas.**

2. Both brother and sister have high **foreheads.**

3. They also have wide **mouths** and pointed **chins.**

4. These are the best years of our **lives.**

5. All the men in my family have glib **tongues.**

B. Traduire le substantif anglais pluriel par un substantif français singulier au sens collectif.

---

pluriel

Modèle: **Americans** are supposed to be materialists.

● ***L'Américain** passe pour matérialiste.*

singulier

---

1. **Englishmen** have the reputation of being stiff and reserved.

2. **Tigers** are carnivorous animals.

3. **Computers** have taken over the business world.

4. **Latins** are reputed to be passionate lovers.

5. **Earthworms** play an important part in ecology.

21 | SUBSTANTIF ANGLAIS / TOURNURE VERBALE FRANÇAISE

A. Traduire le substantif par une construction verbale.

---

adjectif + substantif

Modèle: I rushed into the crowd without **great thought.**

● *Je me suis précipité dans la foule sans **trop penser.***

adverbe + verbe

---

1. His **fervent wish** was to succeed.

2. After **serious consideration,** we agreed to their terms.

3. Her **present plan** is to complete her doctorate and become a college professor.

4. The **unanimous decision** of the committee was to abolish final examinations.

5. If you interrupt him during working hours, you can be sure of a **violent reaction.**

B. Traduire le substantif par une proposition relative.

---

substantif

Modèle: I was able to defend myself against my **attackers.**

- *J'ai pu me défendre contre **ceux qui m'ont attaqué.***

proposition relative

---

1. A good **listener** learns a great deal.

2. **Admirers** of his painting call him the greatest genius of this century.

3. People do not always appreciate hard **workers.**

4. I refuse to pay the **builder** of my house, for he did shoddy work.

5. The poker **players** were totally absorbed in the game.

C. Traduire la préposition + substantif à l'aide d'un gérondif ou d'un participe présent ou passé.

---

préposition + substantif

Modèle: **At the end** of the war, the nation once again had hopes for a better future.

- *La guerre **terminée,** le peuple reprit l'espoir d'un avenir meilleur.*

participe

---

1. **Upon the departure** of the guests, the hostess kicked off her shoes and collapsed on the sofa.

2. **At the start** of the semester, we took a camping trip in the mountains.

3. He entreated them to help him; **after** their **refusal,** he sadly departed.

4. **With a smile,** she countered all objections to her project.

5. **Upon the arrival** of the bus, they shook hands and said goodbye.

---

22 | SUBSTANTIF ANGLAIS / ADJECTIF FRANÇAIS

A. Traduire un des deux substantifs par un adjectif.

---

substantifs

Modèle: At dusk the valley shimmers with **rays of light.**

- *La vallée au crépuscule ondule de **lumière rayonnante.***

substantif + adjectif

---

1. She loves the **noise and bustle of the city.**

2. Whatever happens, she never experiences a **loss of appetite.**

3. He is determined to make up for the **scantiness of his knowledge.**

4. Some children have an **excess of energy.**

5. In the **darkness of night,** I could scarcely see his face.

B. Traduire la préposition + substantif par un adjectif.

---

préposition + substantif
Modèle: **In her youth,** she enjoyed life.

- *Jeune, elle jouissait de la vie.*
  adjectif

---

1. **In her surprise,** she gave vent to a tiny scream.

2. **In his relief,** he uttered a prayer of thankfulness.

3. **In her joy,** she forgot all past hardships and humiliations.

4. **In his days of affluence and power,** he thought only of himself; **in poverty,** he learned compassion.

5. **In sickness,** he sought my help; **after his recovery,** he became my friend for life.

C. Traduire le substantif par l'article *le* + adjectif substantivé.

---

substantif
Modèle: **The extraordinary fact** is that I could do everything.

- *L'extraordinaire, c'est que je pouvais tout faire.*
  le + adjectif

---

1. **The essential thing** is to succeed.

2. Most of us prefer **beauty** to **usefulness.**

3. From the **depths** of his soul, he thanked her.

4. **The best part** of it is that no one will ever know.

5. It is better not to think too much about **the absurdity** of the human condition.

*D. Traduire en employant *d'un* + adjectif substantivé. Noter qu'on laisse sous-entendre un autre adjectif qui traduit l'adverbe anglais.

Modèle: The apartment is **impeccably clean.**

- *L'appartement est **d'un propre!***

  Sous-entendu: *L'appartement est d'une propreté impeccable!*

---

1. The steak was **horribly tough!**

2. The sand is **dazzlingly white.**

3. His work is **exceptionally meticulous!**

4. Her eyes are **incredibly blue!**

5. That young man is **remarkably serious.**

E. Traduire le substantif par l'article partitif *du* + adjectif substantivé.

---

substantif
Modèle: The play has both **good and bad aspects.**

- *La pièce a **du bon et du mauvais.***
  du + adjectif

---

1. There is **truth** in what you say.

2. His work is very uneven; one can find both **genius** and **banality** in it.

3. There is **beauty** in all living creatures.

4. Romantic literature has both **sublime and grotesque sides** to it.

5. That's a **fine way to behave!** (*ironique*)*

F. Traduire les mots en caractères gras par un adjectif comparatif substantivé.

Modèle: I leave this work to **someone more practical and sensible** than I.

- *Je laisse ce travail à **plus entendu** que moi.*

---

1. **A lazier man** than my brother does not exist.

2. You cannot find **a more stubborn person** than he.

3. She knows **someone smarter** than she.

4. There is no **greater Don Juan** than that man!

5. One doesn't often come across **a more gullible individual** than you!

G. Traduire les mots en caractères gras par un adjectif superlatif substantivé.

Modèle: The meeting will take place **in the darkest part** of the forest.

- *Le rendez-vous est fixé **au plus noir** de la forêt.*

---

1. The desert, **in the middle** of summer, becomes an inferno.

2. **In the depths** of the ocean, one finds strange plants and sea creatures.

3. Along Cornwall's **most desolate** coast there are caves where, it is rumored, buried treasure lies hidden.

4. In a small hut **deep in** the woods dwelled a woodcutter and his family.

5. **In the darkest part** of the jungle lives a tribe of natives totally untouched by the so-called civilized world.

H. Traduire le substantif par *ce qu'il y a de* ou *ce qui est* + adjectif.

substantif   substantif

Modèle: He especially values her **gentleness and tenderness.**

- *Il apprécie surtout **ce qu'il y a de doux et tendre** chez elle.*
ce qu'il y a de + adjectifs

1. She prefers **innocence** to **sophistication.**

2. I particularly like his **simplicity** and **modesty.**

3. The **wonder** is that she endured it for such a long time!

4. Our **astonishment** comes from his not telling us sooner.

5. These two poets are obsessed by the **fleetingness** and **senselessness** of human life.

23 | SUJET-RÉSUMÉ

Traduire les mots en caractères gras par un sujet-résumé + substantif approprié (s'il y a lieu).

Modèle: Purchases, shipments, preparations for departure, **the whole thing** seemed exciting.
- *Achats, envois, préparatifs de départ, **tous ces détails** semblaient passionnants.*

1. Gowns, hats, gloves, slippers, shawls, **all these** had to be carefully packed.

2. Her friends, relatives, neighbors, colleagues, students, **everyone** wished her success and happiness in her new career.

3. Rings, bracelets, necklaces, earrings, **everything** came from the most expensive jeweler in the city.

4. Cars, trucks, buses, motorcycles, **all** were paralyzed in a monster traffic jam.

5. The meats, cheeses, salads, wines—**it all** made his mouth water.

24 | SUBSTANTIFS À ÉVITER

A. Traduire *thing* par un substantif plus fort et plus spécifique.

Modèle: Dawn by the sea: What a splendid **thing!**
- *L'aurore au bord de la mer: quel splendide **panorama!***

1. You have done a very brave **thing.**

2. Then she said an amazing **thing.**

3. I have never heard such a funny **thing.**

4. Then an extraordinary **thing** happened at sea.

5. Excellence is a **thing** to be proud of.

B. Traduire *something* + adjectif par un substantif plus précis, accompagné ou non d'un adjectif.

Modèle: There is **something wonderful** about what she is doing.
- *C'est **une merveille,** ce qu'elle fait.*
  substantif

Modèle: There is **something reassuring** about his gaze.
- *De son regard émane **une lueur rassurante.***
  substantif + adjectif

---

1. There is **something amiable** about her whole demeanor.

2. I sense **something mysterious** in his past.

3. Do you find **something fishy** in his explanation?

4. **Something soft and musical** in her voice bespoke her gracious upbringing.

5. We would appreciate **something cool** to refresh us a bit.

C. Traduire *something* + adjectif par un substantif (précédé d'un article indéfini) + un autre substantif tiré de l'adjectif.

Modèle: We noted **something peaceful** about my mother.
- *On a constaté chez ma mère **un esprit de calme.***
  article indéfini + substantif + autre substantif

---

1. There is **something regal** in her bearing.

2. We detect **something obsequious** in his manner.

3. I find **something plausible** in that argument.

4. There was **something mischievous** about his eyes.

5. Don't you feel **something strange** about this place?

D. Traduire en employant *du* + adjectif.

Modèle: Contemporary cinema contains **something valid and meritorious.**
- *Le cinéma contemporain renferme **du valable et du méritoire.***

---

1. You can discern **something good** and **something bad** in every human being.

2. There is **something true** in what you are saying.

3. The poet's restless spirit is constantly in search of **something new.**

4. There is **something sublime** in the art of music.

5. She finds **something beautiful** in each of her students and **something praiseworthy** in each of their compositions.

E. Traduire *people* par un substantif qui signifie le tout par la partie.

---

le tout

Modèle: Traveling presents no problem to **quick-witted people.**

- *Voyager ne présente aucun problème à **un esprit éveillé.***

la partie

---

1. Marriage is often disillusioning to **romantic people.**

2. **People who are sensitive** are not always easy to live with.

3. **Flighty people** refuse to take life seriously.

4. They are **good, worthy people.**

5. **Strong-minded people** are seldom popular with their peers.

F. Traduire *people* par un substantif qui signifie la partie par le tout.

---

la partie

Modèle: **The city** (The people of the city) rejoices at spring's arrival.

- *La **ville** se réjouit à l'arrivée du printemps.*
  le tout

---

1. **The people** were pleased with the results of the presidential election.

2. A scandal shocked **the people of the village.**

3. He received a standing ovation from **the people in the theater.**

4. All **the people in her class** appreciated her dedication.

5. Exceptional hospitality marks **the people in this house.**

Exercices de sélection

Pour tous ces exercices, discuter et comparer vos choix.

A. (20, 21, 24) Traduire le substantif par au moins deux expressions différentes.

Modèle: **The French people** are reputed to be haughty.

- *Le **Français** est censé être hautain.*
- *Les **Français** sont censés être hautains.*
- *Le **peuple français** est censé être hautain.*
- *L'**âme française** est censée être hautaine.*
- *La **France** est censée être une nation d'orgueilleux.*

1. **The American people** are said to be arrogant and materialistic.

2. **Scots** have the reputation of being thrifty.

3. **The people of Paris** appreciate good cooking.

4. Great economic progress has been made in recent years by **the Chinese people.**

5. **Scandalmongers** are, in my opinion, empty-headed **people** who have nothing better to do.

6. I, personally, find **dreamers** more attractive than **thinkers.**

7. **Southerners** have a reputation for being open and hospitable.

8. **Bretons** are generally believed to be devoutly religious **people.**

9. Obviously, **hikers** and **bikers** get more exercise than **drivers.**

10. Patriotism is a known characteristic of **the Polish people.**

B. (19, 21, 22, 24) Traduire le substantif par au moins deux constructions ou formules différentes.

Modèle: He appreciates the beautiful **things** in life.

- *Il apprécie **ce qui est beau** dans la vie.*
- *Il apprécie **le beau** dans la vie.*
- *Il apprécie **la beauté** de la vie.*
- *Il apprécie **les beautés** de la vie.*
- *Il apprécie **ce qu'il y a de beau** dans la vie.*
- *Il apprécie **le beau côté** de la vie.*

1. **In his haste,** he forgot the essential **thing.**

2. **In his youth,** he did many adventurous **things.**

3. There are **good things** and **bad things** in this film.

4. **In her surprise,** she sprang to her feet, knocking over her wine glass and her chair.

5. She wishes to forget the painful **things** in life and to remember only **the beautiful.**

6. She accepted the **kindness** of her neighbors gratefully.

7. He did a most generous **thing.**

8. The important **thing** is to behave maturely.

9. **In adversity,** we learned to appreciate many **things** that we had, **in our** former **happiness,** taken for granted.

10. For example, we found music to be one of the most comforting **things** in life.

C. (21, 22, 23, 24)   Traduire le substantif par au moins deux constructions ou formules différentes.

Modèle: I rushed into the crowd without **great thought.**

- *Je me suis précipité dans la foule sans **trop penser.***
- *Je me suis précipité dans la foule sans **réflexion.***
- ***Étourdi,** je me suis précipité dans la foule.*
- *Je me suis précipité dans la foule **à l'étourdie.***

---

1. She strode away without a **backward glance.**

2. Their **only wish** is to see their children successful and happy.

3. We acted without **serious concern** for consequences.

4. These exercises are **horribly difficult work!**

5. What is the **shortest route** from New York to Atlanta?

6. You cannot find a **more generous person** than he.

7. There was **something noble and majestic** in his bearing.

8. **At the end of the school year,** I began work on a new research project.

9. We find **something foolhardy** in his determination to break all existing records.

10. Love, marriage, children—**the whole thing** can conflict with an ambitious woman's career!

Exercices de synthèse

A. Sur une feuille séparée, traduire les phrases suivantes en utilisant les techniques suggérées dans le chapitre consacré au substantif.

1. Peasants are naturally practical; the cultivation of living things keeps them in touch with earthly realities.
2. At the close of her greatest speech, she said to me in a whisper, "There is something good about fame, after all."
3. Anyone with a clear intellect will easily outwit such clumsy liars.
4. My two colleagues usually prefer style to simplicity and propriety.

5. The astonishing thing is that he has never met anyone stronger than himself.
6. If you women will kindly take off your hats and leave your coats in the coatroom, we shall soon find the shortest way to the loges.
7. Loud talkers, careless passers-by, reckless drivers, and excessive drinkers—all these detract somewhat from the pleasure of living in a big city.
8. The wisdom of your suggestion proves that we should not have the slightest hesitation in taking advantage of your experience.
9. The room was neat as a pin, but so poor, so wretched.*
10. There was a certain indefinable vagueness in his ideas, and after his defeat he realized it.
11. The funniest part of it is that I cannot read those words without blushing.
12. I felt behind the words a masterly gaze and an iron hand.
13. Pride is a dangerous thing; you should strive toward something more lofty.
14. For twenty years she has always talked with a frown; now her forehead is covered with wrinkles.
15. In his discouragement, he was not even doing his best, but after he was cured, he thanked us for our assistance.
16. As I wandered in the darkest part of the forest, I could no longer see the whiteness of the clouds against the blueness of the sky.
17. He was a tireless traveler, and his travels had the uncertainty and strangeness of an adventure.
18. I admitted that this task needed someone better fitted for it than I.
19. The moviegoers of the 1940s have become the television viewers of the 1980s.
20. Among the American people, girl-watchers outnumber bird-watchers ten to one.
21. This thing is too deep for me; I leave it to someone who knows more than I do.
22. With a stifled giggle, the child ran away.
23. At the beginning of her teaching career, her earnest wish was to encourage and influence young people.
24. There is something heroic about attempting a rescue against overwhelming odds!
25. The cathedrals, the museums, the boulevards, the cafés—everything in Nice delighted her.
26. At the end of the war, the conquered nation began to rebuild its shattered economy.
27. We contemplated the moon's silver glow reflected in the deep, calm water.
28. With the arrival of the first robin, we declared the long winter to be officially at an end.
29. The most beautiful thing is that this school is subsidized by the people in the neighborhood; they have been extraordinarily generous!*
30. A more honest man than he does not exist; even the town scandalmongers find it impossible to say anything bad about him!

B. Sur une feuille séparée, traduire ce passage en tenant compte autant que possible des techniques étudiées jusqu'à présent.

> What with the success of her show, of which the notices continued voluminous and uniformly laudatory, and her discovery of Fat Rosa's [café], Martha's final week in Paris opened very comfortably. A third circumstance was that her encounter with her ex-lover, which she would have gone to any lengths to avoid, now that it was over, proved to have been a blessing in disguise. (Martha's reflections on this point so accurately paralleled Mrs. Taylor's, it was only a pity they couldn't exchange congratulations.) Her mistake had lain in attempting to avoid instead of grasping the nettle; upon reflection, Martha felt positively grateful to Eric for taking the initiative and enabling her to get everything finally washed up.
>
> In this new mood of amenity she refrained from either scowling at critics or biting the head off M. Cerisier. The latter, indeed, after the most startling sales in his gallery's records, would almost have offered his head on a platter, and so far flung economy to the winds as to present Martha, at a luncheon *à trois* with *le maître,* the homage of a sizable spray of orchids. Nothing could have been less appropriate to a stout serge lapel—but nothing either, as a testimony of the art-trade's solid interest, more encouraging. . . .
>
> Margery Sharp, *Martha, Eric and George*
> (Boston: Little, Brown, 1964), pp. 137–138.

4 | L'ADJECTIF

Assimilation des structures

A. Traduire l'adjectif par un substantif.

Modèle: That lawyer's reputation is built on **generous** altruism.
adjectif

- *Cet avocat base sa renommée sur **la générosité** et l'altruisme.*
substantif

1. He cultivates an attitude of **ironic** detachment.

2. **Incredulous** delight shone in her eyes.

3. He was so **foolish** as to offend the one person who could have helped him.

4. She has been so **imprudent** as to confide her secret to her friend.

5. The **foolhardy** Houdini attempted perilous stunts that no man had ever accomplished before.

B. Traduire l'adjectif + substantif par deux substantifs liés par la préposition *de.*

Modèle: The **pale dawn** signaled the end of night.
adjectif + substantif

- ***La pâleur de l'aube** signalait que la nuit prenait fin.*
substantif + *de* + substantif

1. The cold wind brightened her **red cheeks.**

2. They walked together through the **shadowy night.**

3. You ought to be proud of this **immaculate house.**

4. The **brilliant sunshine** blinded us for a moment.

5. In the **dark forest,** a solitary owl hooted.

C. Traduire l'adjectif par un substantif (ou un adjectif substantivé) + *de*.

---

            adjectif
Modèle: A **funny** scene took place before us.

   ● *Un **drôle de** spectacle s'est présenté à nos yeux.*
   adjectif
   substantivé + *de*

---

1. What an **adorable** little dog!*

2. **Poor** me! I am so sleepy!

3. She's a **strange** girl; you never know what she will say next.

4. Oh, those **mischievous** green eyes of hers! How they twinkle!

5. A **fine** business this is!

D. Traduire l'adjectif de couleur par *d'un* + adjectif de couleur substantivé.

---

                 adjectif
Modèle: The singer is wearing a dark **green** dress.

   ● *La chanteuse porte une robe **d'un vert** foncé.*
           d'un + adjectif
                 substantivé

---

1. She wore a black coat and a bright **red** hat.

2. The bridesmaids wore pale **pink** gowns and the ushers had on light **blue** jackets.

3. A brilliant **orange** moon shone in the sky.

4. She had dark **brown** hair and soft **gray** eyes.

5. In the study we hung cheerful **yellow** curtains.

26 | SUBSTANTIF EMPLOYÉ COMME ADJECTIF EN FRANÇAIS

A. Traduire l'adjectif par un substantif en apposition utilisé comme adjectif ou par deux substantifs liés par une préposition.

Modèle: She enjoyed using **substandard** expressions.

   ● *Elle se plaisait à employer des expressions **peuple.***
                      substantif adjectivé

Modèle: She leads the most **domestic** existence possible.

- *Elle mène une vie tout ce qu'il y a de plus **pot-au-feu.***
                                                        substantif
                                                        + préposition
                                                        + substantif

1. She is somewhat **scatterbrained** for a **model** employee!

2. The community's **guiding** principle proved not especially innovative.

3. This is a **key** sentence that reveals important ideas of his work.

4. Those **di Camerino** dresses make a **stupendous** impression!

5. She has very **down-to-earth** ideas about married life.

B. Traduire l'adjectif de couleur par un substantif adjectivé invariable.

                                                        adjectif
Modèle: That old woman's hat is trimmed with **plum-colored** ribbons.

- *Des rubans **prune** ornent le chapeau de cette vieille dame.*
        substantif
        adjectivé

1. Those **orange** gloves look hideous with that **salmon-pink** dress!

2. Her **hazel** eyes flashed with anger.

3. The living room drapes were **maroon** with **pistachio** tassels.

4. She wore a ravishing dressing gown of **peach-colored** silk.

5. The twin sisters are wearing **burgundy** wool suits with **turquoise-blue** blouses.

27 | ADJECTIF ANGLAIS / COMPLÉMENT FRANÇAIS INTRODUIT PAR UNE PRÉPOSITION

Traduire l'adjectif par un complément introduit par une préposition.

                                                        adjectif
Modèle: I would like you to see my **favorite** films.

- *Je me permets de vous faire voir mes films **de prédilection.***
                                        complément introduit par une préposition

1. The large windows commanded a view of **English-style** gardens and terraces.

2. A **random** remark revealed that we had attended the same university.

3. Their **town** house boasts an imposing **spiral** staircase.

4. You seem **cheerful** today!

5. Formal evening dress is **customary.**

---

28 | ADJECTIF ANGLAIS / CONSTRUCTION VERBALE FRANÇAISE

A. Traduire l'adjectif en *-ing* par une proposition relative.

---

                         adjectif

Modèle: With a **hesitating** step, she came toward us.

   • *D'un pas **qui bésitait,** elle s'approcha de nous.*
               proposition
               relative

---

1. In a **booming** voice, he exhorted his audience to repent.

2. Her **trembling** hands betrayed her emotion.

3. I cradled the **sobbing** child in my arms.

4. Arriving at the bus stop, we found a long line of **waiting** passengers.

5. According to Blaise Pascal, man is a "**thinking** reed."

B. Traduire l'adjectif marquant le temps par une proposition relative.

---

                         adjectif

Modèle: In their **present** condition, these houses will collapse.

   • *Dans l'état **où elles sont,** ces maisons vont s'effondrer.*
               proposition
               relative

---

1. The **present** century is an era of technological progress.

2. The antecedent of these pronouns can be found in the **preceding** sentence.

3. The **subsequent** paragraph develops an essential theme.

4. She should not drive in her **present** state.

5. The **following** day brought a new, even more interesting opportunity.

C. Traduire le participe (présent ou passé) par une préposition + substantif.

---

                       participe

Modèle: Would you like to buy a **used** car?

   • *Voudriez-vous acheter une voiture **d'occasion?***
                    préposition + substantif

---

1. Will you have **baked** or **mashed** potatoes?

2. French vocabulary is made up, in great part, of **borrowed** words.

3. Stroking her hair, he murmurs **loving** words into her ear.

4. At this season, you can find **reduced-price** merchandise in all the department stores.

5. I enjoy **sunny** days more than **rainy** days.

29 | ADJECTIFS NÉGATIFS

A. Traduire l'adjectif négatif par un verbe négatif + adjectif affirmatif.

---

verbe
affirmatif + adjectif
négatif

Modèle: It **is unthinkable** to speak that way.

- *Il **n'est pas admissible** de parler de la sorte.*

verbe
négatif + adjectif
affirmatif

---

1. She **was unsure** of her welcome.

2. It **would be impossible** to finish this job today.

3. That story **appears absolutely untrue.**

4. Your reaction **seems illogical** to me.

5. Fortunately, the driver and passengers **escaped unharmed.**

B. Traduire l'adjectif négatif par *peu* ou *mal* + adjectif affirmatif.

---

adjectif
négatif

Modèle: I feel **uneasy.**

- *Je me sens **mal à l'aise.***

mal + adjectif
affirmatif

---

1. He proved to be **inexperienced** in automobile repairs.

2. It is **impolite** to stare so obviously.

3. That is an **unusual** situation.

4. She comes across as shy and **unworldly.**

5. They consider it **improbable** that he will get exactly what he wants.

C. Remplacer l'adjectif négatif par *sans* + substantif.

---

adjectif négatif

Modèle: She provokes **endless** discussions.

- *Elle provoque des discussions **sans fin.***

sans + substantif

---

1. She has a warm, **guileless** heart.

2. Look at that lovely, **cloudless** blue sky!

3. They remembered her for her **matchless** beauty.

4. The courtly knight was supposed to be **fearless** and **blameless.**

5. Water is a **colorless, odorless, tasteless** liquid.

D. Remplacer l'adjectif négatif par une proposition relative.

---

adjectif négatif

Modèle: He is a **senseless** individual.

- *C'est un individu **qui n'a pas le sens commun.***

proposition relative

---

1. That remains a **meaningless** sentence.

2. **Careless** students rarely write **faultless** compositions.

3. She is known as a dedicated and **tireless** worker.

4. I pictured marriage as a life of **endless** bliss.

5. She is a well-meaning but **tactless** person.

E. Traduire en évitant les formes comparatives et superlatives de l'adjectif au préfixe négatif.

Modèle: He is **the least dishonest** man in the world!

- *C'est l'homme **le plus honnête** qui soit au monde!*

---

1. She is **less unhappy** now than she was before her marriage.

2. He is not **the clumsiest** boy I have ever seen.

3. They consider city air **unhealthier** than country air.

4. She is **the least unlucky** woman we have ever met.

5. This is **the most difficult** task he has ever accomplished.

30 | ADJECTIFS RENDUS PAR UN ADVERBE

A. Traduire l'adjectif par un complément circonstanciel.

---

                                 adjectif

Modèle: I am the owner of an old **country** house.

    ● *Je suis propriétaire d'une maison ancienne **à la campagne**.*
                                     complément
                                     circonstanciel

---

1. Next year we plan to build an **outdoor** swimming pool.

2. Our doctor lives in a luxurious **suburban** house.

3. Their house contains four **upstairs** bedrooms and a **basement** laundry room.

4. She also maintains a small **city** apartment near the hospital where she works.

5. Many buildings in New York City reveal attractive **roof** gardens.

B. Traduire l'adjectif de temps ou de lieu par *de* + adverbe.

---

                           adjectif

Modèle: I spent the **previous** year in Quebec City.

    ● *J'ai passé l'année **d'avant** à Québec.*
             de + adverbe

---

1. The **"now"** generation refuses to be bound by **yesterday's** rules.

2. I have just met an **old** acquaintance whom I haven't seen for years.

3. The **local** people are not very friendly to strangers.

4. They spent all of June in Paris and the **following** month on the French Riviera.

5. **Today's** schoolchildren will be **tomorrow's** leaders.

C. Traduire l'adjectif par l'adverbe *bien, mal, mieux,* ou *presque, quasi-,* selon le sens.

---

                           adjectif

Modèle: He is an **upstanding** old gentleman.

    ● *C'est un vieux monsieur très **bien**.*
                 adverbe

---

1. That girl is quite **attractive;** she is **better-looking** than her friend.

2. Wouldn't you be **more comfortable** on the sofa, or are you quite **comfortable** where you are?

3. You do not always know what is **right** and what is **wrong.**

4. The **near** unanimity of the vote constitutes a victory for our party.

5. The **almost complete** certitude of winning gave them the strength to continue the struggle.

31 | ADJECTIFS COMPOSÉS

A. Traduire l'adjectif composé par un simple adjectif.

Modèle: She is a **first-class** liar.

- *C'est une **fieffée** menteuse.**

---

1. He made a **halfhearted** attempt to restrain her.

2. She manages to produce thirty **handwritten** pages each day.

3. We ordered **hard-boiled** eggs and a **medium-rare** steak with **french-fried** potatoes.

4. He is reputed to be a **free-spoken, openhanded** man.

5. I am neither **nearsighted** nor **farsighted**; I am **color-blind.**

B. Traduire l'adjectif composé par une locution adjective contenant *de* ou *à*.

---

adjectif composé
Modèle: The spectator experiences a **deep-rooted** emotion.

- *Le spectateur ressent une émotion **aux racines profondes**.*
locution avec *à*

---

1. Her beauty is but **skin-deep.**

2. The usherettes wore **sea-green** dresses.

3. A **tenderhearted** girl, she shrank from hurting others.

4. I saw a **weak-minded** old man sitting on a bench, feeding pigeons.

5. The painter carefully blends **zinc-white** and **cobalt-blue** paint on his palette.

C. Traduire l'adjectif composé par une simple transposition.

---

adjectif 1 + adjectif 2
Modèle: The actor put on a **lemon-yellow** jacket.

- *Le comédien se vêtit d'une veste **jaune citron**.*
adjectif 2 + adjectif 1

---

1. Her **jade-green** silk dress brought out the green of her eyes.

2. She carried a bouquet of **blood-red** flowers.

3. He wore a **navy-blue** suit, a pale yellow shirt, and an **emerald-green** tie.

4. A **pearl-gray** cape enveloped her slender form.

5. Those blue draperies clash horribly with that **olive-green** carpet!

D. Traduire l'adjectif composé en *-ing* par un simple adjectif.

---

adjectif composé
Modèle: We heard a **spine-tingling** noise.
- *On entendit un bruit **terrifiant.***
simple adjectif

---

1. He claims to be a **hard-working** student.

2. Before the invention of machinery, ploughing was **backbreaking** labor.

3. Lulu has an **eye-catching** walk.

4. The president delivered a **soul-stirring** speech.

5. He uttered a **heartrending** revelation.

E. Traduire l'adjectif composé d'abord par une proposition relative, ensuite par *à* + infinitif.

Modèle: You find there a **breathtaking** beauty.
- *Il y a là une beauté **qui vous coupe le souffle.***
- *Il y a là une beauté **à vous couper le souffle.***

---

1. One can find a **soul-stirring** landscape there.

2. Suddenly an **ear-splitting** cry is heard.

3. She began a **soul-searching** study of herself.

4. I am reading a **hair-raising** ghost story.

5. The violins played a soft, sad gypsy melody—a **heartrending** sound.

F. Traduire l'adjectif composé par *d'allure, d'apparence, d'aspect, à l'air, à mine* + adjectif.

---

adjectif composé
Modèle: My neighbor is rather **haughty-looking.**
- *Ma voisine est **d'allure** plutôt **hautaine.***
d'allure + adjectif

---

1. The landlord was a stocky, **fierce-looking** man.

2. Although **shy-looking,** your sister works in many civic associations.

3. I became aware that I was being stared at by an **attractive-looking** stranger.

4. **Harassed-looking** travelers mobbed the waiting room.

5. Two **cheerful-looking** mothers were waiting for their children in front of the school playground.

G.   Traduire en employant l'expression *avoir l'air,* en faisant l'accord de l'adjectif avec *air* ou avec le sujet, selon le sens.

Modèle: She **looks intelligent.**

- *Elle **a l'air intelligent(e)**.*

1. They **appear satisfied.**

2. She **seems surprised.**

3. The spectators **seemed deeply moved.**

4. She and her friend **look puzzled.**

5. My mother **appeared calm and happy.**

H.   Traduire l'adjectif composé par un simple adjectif.

Modèle: We sell only **fresh-picked** vegetables.

- *Nous ne vendons que des légumes **frais**.*

1. They are extremely **well-read.**

2. The meek, long-suffering wife is a **time-worn** stereotype.

3. Fortunately, their happiness was **long-lived.**

4. She represents only **well-known** writers.

5. He wore a **double-breasted** overcoat.

I.   Traduire l'adjectif composé par un participe passé + préposition + substantif.

adjectif   composé
Modèle: In France one often sees **poplar-lined** roads.

- *En France on voit souvent des routes **bordées de peupliers**.*

participe
passé   + *de* + substantif

1. She wore a **sable-lined** coat to the ball.

2. Her **lace-trimmed** chiffon gown cost over a thousand dollars.

3. We walked in silence under a **star-studded** sky.

4. The **fruit-laden** branches hung almost to the ground.

5. They ordered **mocha-flavored** ice cream in a small **smoke-filled** café.

J. Traduire l'adjectif composé par un complément déterminatif introduit par *à*, *de* ou *en*.

---

adjectif composé

Modèle: People formerly wore **horn-rimmed** glasses.

● *Les gens, autrefois, portaient des lunettes **à monture en corne.***
   complément déterminatif

---

1. The **white-veiled** bride advanced gracefully toward the altar.

2. A tall, **red-haired** young fellow stepped forward.

3. We are looking for a **medium-sized** car.

4. A trio of **mink-coated** ladies entered the restaurant chatting gaily.

5. I need a **brocade-covered** armchair.

---

32 | ADJECTIF POSSESSIF ANGLAIS / PROPOSITION RELATIVE FRANÇAISE

A. Traduire l'adjectif possessif par une proposition relative.

---

adjectif
possessif

Modèle: **His** love for me resembles the great loves of antiquity.

● *L'amour **qu'il me voue** ressemble aux grandes amours de l'antiquité.*
   proposition relative

---

1. I accepted **her** offer to accompany me.

2. **Our** era is one of affluence and progress.

3. **His** thesis on the romantic poets shows original insights.

4. In **your** state of health, you should not drink or smoke.

5. **My** certainty that I was right appears to have been unjustified.

B. Traduire le substantif anglais au possessif par une proposition relative.

Modèle: **Stendhal's** book on Rossini is a sheer delight.

● *Le livre **qu'a écrit Stendhal** au sujet de Rossini est une pure merveille.*

---

1. In our **grandparents'** era, life was simpler.

2. **Paul's** new wardrobe was outrageously expensive.

3. Your **brother's** condition appears quite satisfactory.

4. **Mozart's** music is incomparably beautiful.

5. I believe that our **descendants'** lives will be unimaginably complex.

33 EMPLOIS IDIOMATIQUES DE L'ADJECTIF POSSESSIF

A. Traduire en employant le verbe *sentir* et l'adjectif possessif *son, sa, leur.*

Modèle: That woman speaks with an accent very **typical of** New England.
- *Cette femme parle avec un accent qui **sent** tout à fait **sa** Nouvelle-Angleterre.*

1. He speaks with an intonation wholly **characteristic of** Provence.

2. Her values and her attitudes all **smack of** a bourgeois upbringing.

3. Their manners and morals **reek of** the small provincial town.

4. She displays an elegance that **exudes** Paris.

5. His vocabulary and pronunciation **are typical of** Normandy.

B. Traduire en employant l'adjectif possessif dans certaines expressions stéréotypées.

Modèle: She was stretched **full length** on the bed taking a nap.
- *Étendue **de tout son long** sur le lit, elle faisait un petit somme.*

1. He **gets on his high horse** at the slightest provocation.

2. She considered the contest an opportunity to **prove herself.**

3. This is the first time in years that this hungry man has **eaten and drunk his fill.**

4. I cannot believe that she is **in her right mind!**

5. They **did their best** to convince us.

C. Traduire en employant le pronom possessif sans article (le pronom sert ici d'adjectif).

Modèle: I made these properties **my own.**
- *Ces propriétés, je les ai faites **miennes.***

1. After marriage, your wife's financial obligations will be **your own.**

2. I have made this house **my own,** and it will remain **my own.**

3. She considers their children **her own.**

4. After so many years, our neighbors' problems have become **our own.**

5. He regards my family as **his own.**

34 EMPLOIS DIVERS DE L'ADJECTIF DÉMONSTRATIF

A. Traduire l'article défini par l'adjectif démonstratif.

article défini
Modèle: They do not agree with **the** importance you give to the project.
  • *Ils ne l'admettent pas, **cette** importance que vous accordez au projet.*
        adjectif
        démonstratif

1. **The** enthusiasm Professor Legrand generates in his classes is truly remarkable.

2. **The** car you sold me is a real lemon!*

3. **The** black clouds on the horizon mean that stormy weather is coming our way.

4. Everyone should pay close attention, especially **the** students interested in translation courses.

5. **The** collection of poems we are studying today constitutes a highly imaginative exploration of the possibilities of language.

B. Traduire en employant l'adjectif démonstratif pour témoigner de la déférence ou pour indiquer une attitude émotive.

Modèle: Ladies and gentlemen, would you please be seated; the show is about to begin.
  • *Que **ces** messieurs et **ces** dames veuillent bien prendre leurs places, le spectacle commence.*

Modèle: Dear aunt, the children miss her tremendously.
  • ***Cette** chère tante, elle manque énormément aux enfants.*

1. Poor child, he is shivering and his teeth are chattering!

2. Young ladies, would you please come forward?

3. Good old Louise, we can always count on her.

4. We have just written to **the** Duvals, who were so kind to us during our stay in Lyon.

5. Dear cousin George gave me such a generous gift.

C. Traduire l'adjectif démonstratif par un article défini.

---

               adjectif
               démonstratif
               (valeur généralisante)

Modèle: I admire **those** people who, while remaining authentically themselves, still have consideration for other people.

- *J'admire **les** personnes qui, tout en demeurant authentiquement soi, ne manquent pas d'égards*
               article
               défini
               (sens général)
envers autrui.

---

1. **Those** professors who repeat the same old lectures from year to year are usually boring and bored.

2. I can't endure **those** male chauvinists who make sweeping generalizations about women.

3. **Those** drivers who drive while under the influence of alcohol or drugs cause many serious accidents.

4. **Those** individuals who smoke more than one pack of cigarettes per day undoubtedly endanger their health.

5. It seems that **those** buildings erected fifty years ago were constructed far more sturdily than their modern counterparts.

D. Traduire en employant l'adjectif démonstratif avec une valeur particularisante, soit après *de*, soit devant *que*.

Modèle: Alas! Life has **such** moments!

- *Hélas! la vie a de **ces** moments!*

Modèle: I must admit **the** fact that my brother never forgets my birthday.

- *Je dois vous avouer **ce** fait que mon frère n'oublie jamais mon anniversaire.*

---

1. We do not agree with **the** idea that work is a necessary evil.

2. She has **such** adventures!

3. I find **the** thought that life has no meaning totally unacceptable.

4. We sometimes have **such** nightmares!

5. Do you believe in **the** old saying that love conquers all?

E. Traduire en omettant le pronom démonstratif *celui, celle,* entre le verbe *être* et un complément introduit par *de*.

Modèle: He was thirty years old and yet his face was **that of** an adolescent.

- *Il avait trente ans et pourtant son visage semblait être **d'**un adolescent.*

               être + *de* (pronom démonstratif omis)

---

1. Her behavior is **that of** a spoiled child, not of a well-brought-up young lady.

2. His tastes were **those of** a cultured man, not of a laborer.

3. She is over sixty years old, but her bearing is **that of** a woman of thirty.

4. Sir, your manners are hardly **those of** a gentleman!

5. Her gestures and attitudes were **those of** a great woman.

35 | LES ADJECTIFS ANTÉPOSÉS

A. Traduire l'adjectif par un adjectif antéposé, précédé d'un adjectif possessif.

Modèle: Please accept **our heartfelt sympathy.**
   • *Veuillez agréer **nos sincères condoléances.***

1. **His untoward suggestion** pleased none of the directors.

2. I read **your excellent article** with much interest.

3. **Her amazing progress** delighted her teachers.

4. If you ask me, **his so-called intelligence** is only a myth!

5. **Their happy news** delighted us all.

B. Faire précéder l'adjectif lorsque le substantif est suivi d'un complément déterminatif (*de* + substantif ou infinitif). Sentir l'équilibre rythmique de la phrase.

Modèle: We are blessed with **radiant summer days.**
   • *Nous jouissons de **radieuses journées d'été.***
                                   complément déterminatif

1. The child cast toward him **luminous looks of astonishment.**

2. We experienced **joyous evenings during vacation.**

3. **Lovely operatic arias** filled the amphitheater.

4. A **crazy urge to burst out laughing** impelled me to run away.

5. They had the **happy idea of picnicking** beside a **magnificently beautiful waterfall.**

36 | LES ADJECTIFS POSTPOSÉS

A. Traduire l'adjectif par un adjectif postposé. Sentir la valeur différenciatrice de cet adjectif, la disjonction rythmique et sémantique (deux groupes de sens).

Modèle: The general was a **tall man.**
   • *Le général était un **homme grand.***

1. He put on a **gray jacket** and a **clean shirt.**

2. We ate a **succulent meal** in a **Japanese restaurant.**

3. The **indigent old man** was too proud to accept **financial assistance.**

4. They have conducted a **serious study** of **contemporary literature.**

5. He placed the **square-cut diamond** on her **slender finger.**

B. Traduire l'adjectif par un adjectif modifié par un adverbe de plus de deux syllabes.

Modèle: Her fiancé is an **extremely handsome** man.
- *Son fiancé est un homme **extrêmement beau.***

1. He became an **exceptionally able** surgeon.

2. A **horribly difficult** examination awaited us.

3. Laura is an **unusually shy, sensitive** child.

4. He is recognized as an **outstandingly brilliant** scholar.

5. Despite an **overly indulgent** mother, Paul is a likable young man.

C. Traduire en faisant suivre l'adjectif dans une construction absolue ou lorsqu'il s'agit d'un substantif adjectivé.

Modèle: I stared **open-mouthed** at her jewels; that diamond tiara made a **stupendous** impression.
- *Je regardais **bouche bée** ses bijoux; cette tiare diamantée faisait un effet **bœuf.*** *

1. **With bowed head,** the young minister prayed for guidance.

2. Her **brown** eyes have a **youthful** twinkle.

3. She looked at me **with wide-open eyes.**

4. She wore a **cherry-red** silk dress with **straw-colored** ribbons.

5. **With a light heart,** I embarked on the most extraordinary adventure of my life.

D. Traduire en employant la construction *avoir* + *le (la, les)* + substantif + adjectif postposé.

Modèle: This lecturer **has a soft and melodious voice.**
- *Cette conférencière **a la voix douce et mélodieuse.***

1. Marianne **has light brown hair and brown eyes.**

2. The pirate **had a swarthy complexion and piercing black eyes.**

3. Pierre **has a Roman nose.**

4. The twins **have long legs and broad shoulders.**

5. The model **had pale cheeks, scarlet lips, and a long, willowy body.**

---

37 | LES ADJECTIFS À POSITION VARIABLE

A. Traduire en plaçant l'adjectif soit avant, soit après le nom propre.

Modèle: The **solemn Marcel** is interested only in the literature of **ancient Greece.**

- *Le **grave Marcel** ne s'intéresse qu'à la littérature de la **Grèce antique.***

---

1. The **masterful Elizabeth** ruled England for forty-five years.

2. We took a trip to **Central America.**

3. The **fascinating Héloïse** fell in love with her tutor, the **learned Abélard.**

4. The scenery of **rural England** has remained unspoiled.

5. The **witty François-Marie Arouet** wrote his works under the name Voltaire.

B. Traduire l'adjectif par un adjectif antéposé. Sentir la valeur affective de cet adjectif, l'unité rythmique et sémantique.

Modèle: Thomas Jefferson was a **great man.**

- *Thomas Jefferson était un **grand homme.***

---

1. My **poor sister** tried to get a tan and got a sunburn.

2. He is a **real friend!**

3. My **former employer** is a great guy!*

4. His **latest book** is a **truly outstanding success.**

5. Dreamily, she watched the **white snow** falling.

C. Traduire les adjectifs en caractères gras.

Modèle: Who is that **slim** woman in the **black** dress?

- *Qui est cette femme **mince** à la robe **noire?***

Modèle: What **astounding** films Fellini's are!

- *Quels **époustouflants** films que ceux de Fellini!* *

---

1. This has been a **rigorous** winter with **heavy** snow and **strong** winds.

2. What a **marvelous** show!

3. For the first course they served **cold** tuna with a **delectable** mayonnaise.

4. That **old** fool has made an **incredible** blunder.

5. This **truly admirable** woman has proved a **sincere** friend to us all.

D. Modifier la phrase de façon à éliminer le heurt de certains sons vocaliques.

Modèle: Regardez le *chat allongé* sur le lit.
- *Regardez le **chat étiré** (**étendu**) sur le lit.*

1. C'est une *enfant ambitieuse.*

2. L'auteur raconte les exploits d'un *héros audacieux.*

3. Cet homme est un *vrai épicurien.*

4. C'est une *revue unique.*

5. Où est ce *chien insupportable?*

E. Traduire chaque phrase deux fois, en mettant l'adjectif d'abord à sa place normale, ensuite dans une position insolite. Apprécier la valeur affective de l'adjectif déplacé.

Modèle: His first film was an **outstanding** success.
- *Son premier film a été une réussite **prodigieuse**.*
          position normale

Modèle: His first film was a (truly) **outstanding** success.
- *Son premier film a été une **prodigieuse** réussite.*
          position insolite

1. This is a **pleasant** surprise! This is a (most) **pleasant** surprise!

2. What an **unfortunate** mistake! What a (truly) **unfortunate** mistake!

3. She is an **excellent** student. She is a (really) **excellent** student.

4. They bought a **huge** car. They bought a (really) **huge** car.

5. He takes pleasure in being a **charming** person. He takes pleasure in being a (downright) **charming** person.

F. Traduire en employant les adjectifs *aucun* et *seul* en position inhabituelle pour souligner leur valeur affective.

Modèle: No matter how influential that man appears, he has in fact **no** power **whatever.**

● *Cet homme a beau paraître influent, il est en réalité **sans** puissance **aucune.***

Modèle: By the **sheer** will to live she made a complete recovery.

● *Par sa **seule** volonté de vivre, elle recouvra la santé.*

1. He succeeded brilliantly in his studies **without the slightest** effort.

2. In the National Library **alone** you find a great number of priceless manuscripts.

3. **Without any** talent **whatsoever,** by dint of perseverance **alone,** he became a multimillionaire.

4. Pride **alone** prevented him from abandoning his project.

5. She faced the future **without the slightest apprehension.**

G. Traduire en employant le procédé dit chiasme.

Modèle: She possesses both an **exceptional intelligence** and an **exquisite sensitivity.**

● *Il existe chez elle une **intelligence exceptionnelle** et une **exquise sensibilité.***
             substantif + adjectif   adjectif + substantif

Modèle: An **old castle** and a **modern building** face each other in the same village.

● *Un **vieux château** et un **bâtiment moderne** se font face dans le même village.*
   adjectif + substantif   substantif + adjectif

1. Within that **frail body** dwells a **powerful mind.**

2. We observed with amusement a **tiny mother** with an **enormous daughter** in tow.

3. He is a **loving father** and a **generous husband.**

4. She combines both **impeccable beauty** and **impeccable taste.**

5. My sister possesses a **soft voice** and a **gentle nature.**

H. Expliquer la place de l'adjectif dans les exemples suivants.

1. une fausse fenêtre; une fenêtre étroite

2. une charmante promenade; une agréable surprise

3. de tardives remontrances; des fruits tardifs

4. un nouveau marié; du vin nouveau

5. un secret désir; une porte secrète

6. de rares clients; de rares cheveux; un livre rare

7. un anneau nuptial; le parti républicain

8. une sublime religion; la religion catholique

9. un étrange animal; un animal boîteux

10. un clocher pointu; du vin blanc; de noirs soucis

11. les notes hautes; les notes basses (d'un instrument); la haute mer; le Haut-Limousin; la Basse-Auvergne; les Pays-Bas

12. un dévot personnage; un triste père; un père triste

13. un méchant livre; un livre méchant; un franc imbécile; un ami franc

14. un maigre dîner; un dîner maigre

15. la fausse gloire; un calcul faux; un faux ami; un homme faux; une pierre fausse; un faux nom; une fausse clé

Exercices de sélection

Pour tous ces exercices, discuter et comparer vos choix.

A. (25, 26, 27) Traduire les mots en caractères gras par au moins deux constructions ou expressions différentes.

Modèle: The manager, quite proud, showed us **his spotless building.**
- *Le régisseur nous faisait voir, tout fier, **la propreté de son local.***
- *Le régisseur, tout fier, nous faisait voir **son local immaculé.***
- *Tout fier, le régisseur nous faisait voir **son local sans tache.***
- *Le régisseur nous faisait voir, tout fier, **son local qui était d'une propreté irréprochable.***

---

1. She believes that she leads an **irreproachable life.**

2. The schoolgirls were wearing **dark blue uniforms.**

3. He is a **strange boy;** he tries to hide his true feelings.

4. The clergyman had twinkling eyes and a **good-natured smile.**

5. We wandered for hours in the **dark forest.**

6. The dowager wore a **purplish red** gown and a **mustard-colored** turban.

7. His **favorite book** was Napoleon's *Mémorial de Sainte-Hélène.*

8. My professional and personal life congealed into a **meaningless routine.**

9. You are looking **cheerful** this morning!

10. It is **customary** to knock before entering.

B. (28, 29, 30) Traduire l'adjectif par au moins deux constructions ou expressions différentes.

Modèle: The secretary speaks to me in a **quavering** voice.
- *La secrétaire me parle d'une voix **qui tremblote (qui chevrote)**.*
- *La secrétaire me parle d'une voix **tremblotante (chevrotante)**.*
- *La secrétaire me parle d'une voix **pleine de trémolos**.*
- *La secrétaire me parle **avec des trémolos** dans la voix.*

1. She amused us with her **endless** chatter.

2. Increasing social consciousness marks the **present** era.

3. We experienced a lot of trouble with that **secondhand** car we bought.

4. A **very attractive** woman stepped into the office.

5. That young man seems nervous and **insecure.**

6. Everyone calls her a **harmless, blameless,** totally **selfless** person.

7. One **urban** apartment costs more than three **country** houses.

8. Where were you on the **previous** night?

9. **Yesterday's** irresponsible waste is the cause of **today's** energy crisis and, quite possibly, **tomorrow's** reduced standard of living.

10. He has shown himself **far from unworthy** of our trust.

C. (31) Traduire l'adjectif composé par au moins deux constructions ou expressions différentes.

Modèle: It is a **soul-stirring** event.
- *C'est un événement **qui vous remue l'âme**.*
- *C'est un événement **à vous remuer l'âme**.*
- *C'est un événement **émouvant**.*

1. It is a **heartrending** sight.

2. She put on a leather coat and **fur-lined** gloves.

3. The **black-gowned** woman wore no jewelry except for a single **pear-shaped** diamond sparkling on her breast.

4. She utters an **eyebrow-raising** remark.

5. The **red-haired** child ran away laughing.

6. A **heroic-looking** actor played the role of the captain.

7. They raised their **wine-filled** glasses in a silent toast.

8. Her white satin slippers glittered with **diamond-studded** heels.

9. He sports a **gold-trimmed** tuxedo.

10. Those jet planes make an **ear-splitting** din.

D. (32, 33, 34) Traduire les mots en caractères gras de deux façons différentes.

Modèle: **His love for me** resembles the great loves of antiquity.
- *L'amour qu'il me voue ressemble aux grandes amours de l'antiquité.*
- *Cet amour qu'il éprouve pour moi ressemble aux grandes amours de l'antiquité.*

---

1. To the caveman, **our** present time would seem bewildering.

2. **His** era was more primitive and therefore less complex.

3. **Montaigne's** essay on friendship deserves its fame.

4. The butcher spoke in an accent **characteristic** of Marseilles.

5. When he had eaten and drunk **his fill,** he began to feel sleepy.

6. **The** painting you are admiring represents a striking example of the artist's early work.

7. **The** wine we are drinking is known for its exquisite bouquet.

8. I pity **those** people who do not know how to love.

9. **Those** attitudes we learn in early childhood influence us throughout our lives.

10. **Dearest Denise,** she has always been so kind to us!

E. (35, 36, 37) Traduire en plaçant l'adjectif soit avant, soit après le substantif selon les techniques étudiées. Justifier vos choix.

Modèle: We are blessed with **radiant** summer days.
- *Nous jouissons de **radieuses** journées d'été.*
- *Nous jouissons de journées d'été **radieuses**.*

Justification: le substantif *journées* est suivi d'un complément déterminatif, *d'été;* ainsi, l'adjectif qui précède donne à la phrase un rythme mieux équilibré.

Modèle: Everyone feels sorry for his **poor** wife.

- *Tout le monde a pitié de sa **pauvre** femme.*
- *Tout le monde a pitié de sa femme **pauvre**.*

Justification: le contexte indique que *pauvre* exprime la pitié (impression subjective) plutôt que la misère (caractéristique distinctive); *sa femme pauvre* suggère qu'il a deux femmes, l'une riche, l'autre pauvre; ainsi, l'adjectif doit précéder le substantif.

1. Who is that **truly ravishing** girl?

2. Please accept my **heartfelt** thanks.

3. I watched the **white** snow falling on the rooftops.

4. She received a letter from a **former** student of hers.

5. We had lunch in a **French** restaurant.

6. That professor is reputed to be an **extremely tough** teacher.

7. You made a **big** mistake!

8. How can anyone accept those **ridiculous** ideas of hers?

9. The witch had a **long** nose and a **pointed** chin.

10. We are taking a **superb** course in the literature of **ancient** Greece.

Exercices de synthèse

A. Sur une feuille séparée, traduire les phrases suivantes en utilisant les techniques suggérées dans le chapitre consacré à l'adjectif.

1. A very nice policeman was kind enough to show me the way.
2. His style is very commonplace and his vocabulary rather old-fashioned; it is altogether right that he should be refused the prize.
3. Her head was thrown back and she said, "I am most comfortable here"; frankly, I felt helpless.
4. I felt almost certain that he was the tough-looking fellow that I had met the previous week.*
5. As the hazy moon disappeared behind the copper-colored clouds, we heard a breathtakingly beautiful melody.
6. That is a spiffy little hat; it is the tuft of straw-colored feathers that makes it look so casual.
7. At the present time, and especially in our present condition, borrowed clothes seem fully appropriate.
8. Yesterday's newspaper called his proposal for world peace rather unrealistic.
9. It is unfair to call her a tactless, thoughtless busybody; for my part, I consider her a devoted mother and a loyal friend.
10. It is obvious that a trustworthy servant would not intentionally keep her in such a restless condition.

11. Why did you utter such an ear-splitting scream? It is only a poor, harmless-looking mouse!
12. He makes the most inconvenient plans and the most incorrect statements; he is unworthy of being elected president.
13. She calls him a model husband; as for me, I find him pleasant-looking but rather uninteresting.
14. What a stunning decor! Those pearl-gray drapes go so beautifully with the lemon-yellow walls and the turquoise-blue couch!
15. She offered me some medium-sized, rather unsatisfactory looking pieces, and I have been ill-humored ever since.
16. Above the sloping fields, the sky was a vivid pink, shaded with lilac and iridescent blue.
17. On a rainy night you can hear the water running down the main chimney; I am sure that the house is unhealthy to live in.
18. He stumbles and falls full length; then, when he gets up, he knocks over a Louis XV armchair. He is the clumsiest man I have ever seen!
19. She is not bad-looking; she is better-looking than her brother at any rate, and I think she is very affable.
20. He is usually pretentious, but in a confidential moment, he told me of his humdrum life.*
21. I slept my fill last night, for the first time in weeks.
22. I was quite surprised to read Robbe-Grillet's criticism of Gascar.
23. His father was a carpenter by trade.
24. Will the men be seated; the women can leave their coats in the coatroom.
25. According to her will, after her death her entire library became mine.
26. Those words that add nothing to the sentence may be omitted.
27. Her clothes were elegant and her bearing was regal.
28. Poor Roland thought it was his duty to criticize you in that way.
29. In our times, I admire a statesman who struggles against political treachery.
30. What nerve! And that is nerve! You can sense his plebeian origins as soon as you enter the room.*

B. Sur une feuille séparée, traduire ce passage en tenant compte autant que possible des techniques étudiées jusqu'à présent.

> I wandered around and ended up at my desk, looking at the page that was in my typewriter, specifically page fifty-seven of my brute thesis, my impressions of the novel in France—my big academic lunge. I turned on my lamp, my desk lamp of countless adjustments, and read what there was of page fifty-seven and laughed out loud, but not because it was amusing—because it was such busywork, this whole thing of writing a thesis so that I could become a teacher, particularly when the thesis is about writers, very current ones, women mostly and young, not much older than I am but whom I was exploiting ruthlessly to provide me with a thesis. I'd really have preferred it the other way around, to be myself the writer and have all those others writing their theses about me; but I have a peculiar problem in that my mother was a writer—author of two novels, and three plays, and quite a few screenplays, all quite well known, and it's not easy for the child of a writer to become a writer. I don't see why; it just isn't. It's something about not wanting to be compared. And not wanting to measure up, or not measure up; or cash in either. It's not that I have anything against my mother. I loved her, I think; but my mother's only been dead three years, just short of three years, and I'd rather wait a decent interval and then try. Or not try. But first write the idiotic thesis and get the gap-stopping* degree.
>
> Dorothy Baker, *Cassandra at the Wedding*
> (New York: Signet, 1966), pp. 8–9.

5 | L'ARTICLE

Assimilation des structures

38	EMPLOI ET OMISSION DE L'ARTICLE DEVANT UN SUBSTANTIF EN APPOSITION

A. Traduire en employant l'article devant le substantif en apposition.

Modèle: The painting is by Braque, **the** celebrated French painter (you know).

- *Le tableau est de Braque, **le** célèbre peintre français.*

    article   +   substantif
    défini   en apposition

1. We are going Friday night to hear Arrau, **the** famous pianist (you know).

2. Odile has all her clothes made to order by Cardin, **the** world-renowned designer.

3. This is a bust of Voltaire, **the** eighteenth-century *philosophe*.

4. Houdon, **the** famous sculptor who lived at the time, did the work.

5. We buy our coffee and tea at Vial's, **the** corner grocer.

B. Traduire en omettant l'article devant le substantif en apposition.

Modèle: I buy meat at Caron's, **a** neighborhood butcher.

- *J'achète la viande chez Caron, boucher du quartier.*

    article
    omis

1. He is writing his thesis on the metrical innovations of Baïf, **a** poet of the French Renaissance.

2. He is the son of Jean Duval, **a** professor at the University of Montreal.

3. These croissants are from Dufour's, **a** neighborhood baker.

4. **An** enthusiastic photographer, he carries his camera with him at all times.

5. She was born in 1940, **a** tragic year for France.

C. Traduire en omettant l'article devant le substantif en apposition ou en employant un pronom tonique auxiliaire devant ce substantif.

---

           article

Modèle: **A** faithful observer of American history, he allows nothing to escape him.

   ● *Observateur fidèle de l'histoire américaine, il ne laisse rien lui échapper.*
     article omis

Modèle: **A** faithful observer of American history, he allows nothing to escape him.

   ● *Il ne laisse rien lui échapper, **lui** observateur fidèle de l'histoire américaine.*
               pronom
             (article omis)

---

1. **A** shrewd businesswoman, she became a multimillionaire before she was thirty.

2. **A** devoted mother, she suffered an identity crisis when her youngest son got married.

3. **An** only child, she had a good relationship with her parents.

4. **A** true philanthropist, he has contributed substantially to a number of worthy causes.

5. **A** loyal admirer, she has read all his works.

---

39 | EXPRESSIONS FIGÉES

Traduire en omettant l'article dans l'expression figée.

---

            article   article

Modèle: We will remain **in the city until the beginning** of August.

   ● *Nous resterons **en ville jusqu'à début** août.*
          article   article
          omis   omis

---

1. Zeus visited Danaë **in the form** of a shower of gold.

2. He remained rooted **to the spot** with amazement.

3. She sat down and placed her bundles **upon the ground.**

4. Fortunately, we were not obliged to sell **at a loss.**

5. They left **at the end of May** and returned **on the appointed day.**

40 | ARTICLE DÉFINI ANGLAIS / ARTICLE INDÉFINI FRANÇAIS

A. Traduire l'article défini devant le premier substantif par l'article indéfini; omettre l'article indéfini devant le deuxième substantif.

---

article défini + article indéfini

Modèle: This work reveals **the hand of a master.**

● *Ce travail fait voir **une main de maître.***

article   article
indéfini   omis

---

1. My friend has **the body of an athlete.**

2. She displays **the artlessness of a child.**

3. His hand came down with **the power of a hammer.**

4. Suddenly **the song of a bird** sounded in the silent forest.

5. The young boy had **the face of a snub-nosed angel.**

B. Traduire *as (a), as of, akin to, like a, -like* par cette même structure, article indéfini + substantif + *de* + substantif.

Modèle: In the middle of winter, we had sunny, **springlike weather.**

● *En plein hiver il faisait **un temps** ensoleillé **de printemps.***

article
indéfini + substantif + *de* + substantif

---

1. Candid and trusting, she spoke with **childlike expressions.**

2. During the summer, in an old cabin in the woods, he leads an **existence akin to that of a hermit.**

3. The people in my dream had a **phantomlike insubstantiality** that I found strangely beautiful.

4. At the intersection, a policeman directs traffic with jerky **gestures like a robot's.**

5. The lovely stranger had a **sylphlike body** that fascinated me.

41 | *DE* OU *À* LIANT DEUX SUBSTANTIFS

A. Traduire en omettant l'article devant le deuxième substantif.

Modèle: That is the **east wind** blowing.

● *C'est le **vent d'est** qui souffle.*

de
sans
article

---

1. Have you met the new **Spanish teacher?**

2. Ours is a **watchdog.**

3. In poetry, **plays on words** can reveal hidden meanings.

4. The **wheatfields** gleam under the sun.

5. Is that a **passenger train** or a **freight train?**

B. Traduire en employant l'article devant le deuxième substantif.

Modèle: That is the **north wind** blowing.

   • *C'est le **vent du nord** qui souffle.*
        de + article

---

1. The **tricks of fate** often prove amusing.

2. He devoted his life to medical research for the **love of humanity.**

3. The **study of history** absorbed her totally.

4. Over the city, the **shadow of dusk** gently fell.

5. He has never experienced the **pangs of jealousy.**

C. Traduire en omettant l'article.

Modèle: On Sundays they served wine in a **coffee cup.**

   • *Le dimanche on servait le vin dans une **tasse à café.***
                                    à
                                    sans
                                    article

---

1. Who invented the first **steam engine?**

2. The lute is a **stringed instrument** dating back to ancient times.

3. In the drugstore she bought a **toothbrush** and a **nail file.**

4. On a small table stood a silver decanter and two **wine glasses.**

5. That's a **jewel case,** not a **music box!**

D. Traduire en employant *à* + article défini. Justifier l'emploi de l'article.

Modèle: We ordered **vegetable soup.**

   • *Nous avons commandé un **potage aux légumes.***
                          à + article
   Justification: le deuxième substantif (*légumes*) indique les ingrédients ou composantes du premier (*potage*).

---

1. For dessert they served **chocolate mousse.**

2. Do you know that **woman with the auburn hair?**

3. Over the table hangs a huge, brilliantly colored **oil painting.**

4. She is a **strong-minded professor with a fascinating personality.**

5. Kindly drop these envelopes into the **mailbox.**

E. Traduire en employant la préposition *à;* omettre ou employer l'article. Justifier votre choix.

Modèle: In the bedroom there were four **sash windows.**
- *Dans la chambre il y avait quatre **fenêtres à guillotine.***
  à (article omis)

Justification: les deux substantifs font un tout.

Modèle: The tourists visited the **city of the leaning tower.**
- *Les touristes ont visité la **ville à la tour penchée.***
  à + article

Justification: le substantif dénote un fait censé être connu de tout le monde.

1. For lunch we had **watercress soup** and a **ham sandwich.**

2. My father needs a new **bottle rack.**

3. Look at that ridiculous little **man with the enormous moustache.**

4. She is a **woman with a will of iron.**

5. I dropped my **nail file** in the **clothes chest.**

F. Traduire en utilisant *avec* + article indéfini (ou adjectif possessif).

Modèle: In Venice one sees multicolored houses **with** stucco facades.
- *À Venise on voit des maisons **avec des** façades enduites de stuc et **avec des** couleurs multiples.*

1. The city hall was a squat building **with** bright orange domes.

2. The boy **with a** broken leg stood apart and watched his classmates at play.

3. All along the street one saw cabarets **with** bright neon signs.

4. You will pass a white house **with a** green roof and green shutters.

5. In the living room we have installed a fireplace **with** blue porcelain tiles.

42 | OMISSION DE L'ARTICLE: AUTRES EXEMPLES

A. Traduire en employant *en* sans article pour indiquer la matière dont une chose est faite.

Modèle: She is wearing a **silver bracelet.**
- *Elle porte un **bracelet en argent.***
   en sans
   article

1. They stole a **gold watch** and a **platinum chain.**

2. I packed everything in **cardboard boxes.**

3. We live in a **brick house.**

4. On the table, wine glasses sparkle against a white **linen tablecloth.**

5. An oversized **wooden bookcase** covered one entire wall of the room.

B. Traduire en omettant l'article après *en, en tant que, comme* (*as a, in the capacity of*).

    article
Modèle: He had the audacity to present himself **as a** dancing master.
- *Il a eu l'audace de se présenter **comme** maître de danse.*
   comme
   sans
   article

1. She disguised herself **as a** gypsy.

2. **As a** teacher, he is highly successful.

3. **In the capacity of** museum director, he exerts considerable influence on the art world.

4. She arrived at the costume ball dressed **as a** shepherdess.

5. **In his capacity as** scholar and literary critic, he commands a loyal following.

C. Traduire en omettant l'article devant le substantif en caractères gras. Justifier l'omission de l'article.

Modèle: She left London **at the height of the season.**
- *Elle a quitté Londres **en pleine saison.***
   article
   omis

   Justification: on omet obligatoirement l'article dans l'expression *en plein* + substantif.

1. It's **simple as A, B, C.**

2. Have you ever seen such a hot day **in the middle of winter?**

3. After the wedding—**if there is a wedding**—both families will be able to relax.

4. I have urged him, **many a time,** to trust me.

5. To build a lasting relationship is not **an easy matter.**

D. Traduire en omettant l'article.

Modèle: Throughout the valley **only** rivers and streams could be seen.

● *Dans toute la vallée on **ne** voyait **que** rivières et ruisseaux.*
                                        articles
                                        omis

1. Her victory, **if victory there be,** will give great satisfaction to us all.

2. One would not expect such a dramatic scene **in open court in the middle of the twentieth century.**

3. In the African desert, summer is **but** stifling heat and dryness.

4. That original young designer has just created a suede evening gown that was greeted **with profuse compliments.**

5. **There will** surely **be a way** of finding a hotel room in London **at the height of the season.**

---

43 | EMPLOI DE L'ARTICLE: AUTRES EXEMPLES

A. Traduire en employant l'article défini devant la tournure adjectif + substantif. Noter la valeur exclamative de la tournure.

Modèle: **What a lovely summer** we had!

● *Le bel été qu'on a eu!*
  article
  défini

1. **What an exquisite bouquet** this Beaujolais has!

2. **How frigid winter is** in Canada!

3. That violin has **such a beautiful sound!**

4. **What a nasty man!**

5. **Pretty butterfly!**

B. Traduire en employant *y avoir* ou *tenir* + *de* + article défini devant le substantif.

Modèle: There was **something of the dreamer-poet** about him.

● *Dans son allure, **il y avait du poète rêveur.***

        y avoir + *de* + article
                            défini

1. There is **something of the aristocrat** in her bearing.

2. I thought there was **a bit of the braggart** in his manner.

3. In her walk one senses **something of the seductress.**

4. He **smacks of the jester,** don't you agree?

5. In her reactions, one feels **something old-maidish** and **old hat.**

C. Traduire en employant l'article *des* devant le nombre.

Modèle: It happens that we give a course with **some** forty or fifty students.
  • *Il se trouve que nous faisons un cours avec **des** quarante ou **des** cinquante étudiants.*

---

1. He goes to see his psychiatrist **some** three or four times a week.

2. She spends **a good** twelve hours a day doing research for her novel.

3. We have to spend **about** fifteen thousand dollars for a new car.

4. They still need **around** nine or ten days of concentrated work to revise their introduction.

5. I still have **approximately** fifty pages to complete.

D. Traduire en employant *dans* + article défini pour indiquer la délimitation ou l'approximation.

Modèle: The bank deposits your money **within** twenty-four hours.
  • *La banque dépose votre argent **dans les** vingt-quatre heures.*
            dans + article défini

---

1. Good new cars cost **approximately** fifteen thousand dollars these days.

2. He earns **about** eight hundred francs a week.

3. Her grandmother is **likely** in her seventies now.

4. Please reply **within** ten days.

5. She must weigh **approximately** fifty kilos.

*E. Traduire en employant l'article indéfini devant le substantif abstrait. Noter la valeur affective de l'article.

Modèle: The lawyer made his case with **such eloquence!**
  • *L'avocat a plaidé avec **une éloquence!***
            article + substantif
            indéfini   abstrait

---

1. He has **such nerve!**

2. At departure time, she was **in a rush, let me tell you!**

3. That child behaves with **such poise** and **assurance!**

4. This film **really and truly frightens me!**

5. She is **so kind, so sweet!**

*F. Traduire en employant *d'un* + un adjectif employé comme substantif.

Modèle: The ceremony was **really magnificent!**
- *La cérémonie était **d'un magnifique!***

1. That lecture was **so very erudite!**

2. Her argument was **so lucid!**

3. Their gestures and grimaces were **really comical!**

4. The sky is **so very blue!**

5. His music is **just entrancing!**

Exercices de sélection

Pour tous ces exercices, discuter et comparer vos choix.

A. **(38, 39)** Traduire chaque phrase deux fois, si possible, en faisant varier l'article devant le substantif. Justifier l'emploi ou l'omission de l'article.

Modèle: The painting is by Braque, **the** celebrated French **painter.**
- *Le tableau est de Braque, **le** célèbre **peintre** français.*
- *Le tableau est de Braque, célèbre **peintre** français.*
- *Le tableau est de Braque, **un** célèbre **peintre** français.*

Justification: en disant *the celebrated French painter,* on suppose que le lecteur ou l'auditeur connaît déjà Braque; l'emploi de l'article défini en français (*le célèbre peintre français*) rend de façon très précise cette nuance de sens.

1. I bought this bracelet at Dupont's, **a** neighborhood **jeweler.**

2. **A** dedicated **teacher,** she spends many hours preparing her courses.

3. He will play waltzes, nocturnes, and études by Chopin, **the** famous **composer.**

4. The jockey **dismounted.**

5. **On the appointed day,** I reported to the vice-chancellor's office.

6. She is personally acquainted with Elizabeth Taylor, **the** world-renowned **superstar.**

7. He was made a vice-president, **a promotion** that was long overdue.

8. I will be on vacation until **the end of September.**

9. The devil appeared to Eve **in the guise** of a serpent.

10. **During the week** he lives in a furnished room near the college; on weekends he goes home.

B. (40, 41)   Traduire chaque phrase d'au moins deux façons en faisant varier l'article.

Modèle: We heard near the cabin **the sound of a stream.**
- *Nous entendîmes près de la cabane* **un bruit de ruisseau.**
- *Nous entendîmes près de la cabane* **le bruit d'un ruisseau.**

1. He exhibits **the vitality of a young man.**

2. She acquiesced with **a martyrlike resignation.**

3. He has **the capriciousness of a spoiled child.**

4. **The fragrance of lilacs** filled the air.

5. She has a **fairylike form.**

6. Notice the girl **with the long blond hair and lovely legs.**

7. She gave me an excellent recipe for **pumpkin soup.**

8. Louise has a cat **with beautiful white fur.**

9. Will you get the **milk jug** from the pantry?

10. He is a man **with a keen mind.**

C. (42, 43)   Traduire les mots en caractères gras par au moins deux constructions ou expressions dif-férentes.

Modèle: We can't talk here **right out in the street.**
- *Nous ne pouvons pas parler ici,* **en pleine rue.**
- *Nous ne pouvons pas parler ici,* **au milieu de la rue.**
- *Nous ne pouvons pas parler ici,* **dans la rue.**

1. **There is a possibility** of going to France next summer.

2. Mary had a little lamb, its fleece was **white as snow.**

3. Let us drink some champagne, **if champagne there be.**

4. Look at that impressive **marble** mantelpiece.

5. You have been told **many, many times** to work harder.

6. **What a** nice-looking boy!

7. Actors rehearse **approximately** forty hours per week.

8. He plays his role **with such** fervor, **such** passion!*

9. **There was something of the** Madonna about her.

10. There were **some** five hundred people in the theater.

D. (38, 39, 40, 41, 42, 43) En complétant les phrases suivantes, choisir entre l'emploi et l'omission de l'article. Justifier vos choix.

Modèle: ___(a)___ mouette à ___(b)___ essor mélancolique,
Elle suit la vague, ma pensée . . .

- *Mouette **à l'**essor mélancolique,*
- *Mouette **à** essor mélancolique,*

Justification:

(a) *Omission* — le substantif en apposition *mouette* précède l'autre substantif (*pensée*) et le pronom *elle* qui remplace celui-ci (§**38**.3).
(b) *Emploi* ou *omission* — l'emploi de l'article est facultatif (§**41**.3.B.). Ici on préfère l'emploi à l'omission pour des raisons d'euphonie: l'emploi de l'article évite l'hiatus *à essor*.

Traduction:

A seagull with a mournful glide,
My fancy skims along the wave . . .

---

1. Nous lisons « La Fille à ___(a)___ yeux d'or, » ___(b)___ nouvelle de Balzac.

2. Vous avez sûrement entendu parler de Don Juan, ___(a)___ homme à ___(b)___ femmes notoire.

3. ___(a)___ psychologue fin, Racine n'avait pas d'égal en tant que ___(b)___ chroniqueur des passions humaines.

4. D'habitude froide comme ___(a)___ glace, elle a chanté, ce soir-là, avec ___(b)___ fougue!*

5. Y a-t-il ___(a)___ moyen d'avoir une belle poularde avec des champignons à ___(b)___ crème?

6. Elle a ___(a)___ mine de ___(b)___ déterrée.

7. Ah! ___(a)___ aimable garçon! presque ___(b)___ enfant encore, pensa-t-il.

8. Un renard argenté, d'occasion, va chercher dans ___(a)___ dix mille.

9. Qu'est-ce qu'elle va pouvoir nous faire comme ___(a)___ plat doux, la Tite, une crème à ___(b)___ chocolat, une crème renversée, un flan ou une tarte à ___(c)___ prunes?

10. Assise à sa table préférée, contre une cheminée à ___(a)___ hotte, Hermine commanda un steak à ___(b)___ poivre et de la salade.

Exercices de synthèse

A. Sur une feuille séparée, traduire les phrases suivantes en utilisant les techniques suggérées dans le chapitre consacré à l'article.

1. It is unreasonable to sell at a loss just to pay a bill that is not even due yet!
2. It was an oil painting of an old man with a white beard and long, wrinkled fingers.
3. Not much of an advantage to be noble! As a man of good breeding, you have been behaving more like a vulgar and grouchy boor.
4. At the top of the hill stands the Pantheon, the famous temple of Sainte Geneviève, patron saint of Paris.
5. Our jar of cream got broken this morning; may I borrow a wine-glassful for my mushroom soup?
6. Within twenty-four hours I must try to solve the problem, since there is a problem; it is so very difficult!*
7. A freethinker and an atheist, he did not feel bound by many a convention that confines us ordinary mortals.
8. He had a chubby-cheeked face, like a cherub; I would never have thought he was a big manufacturer with an iron will.
9. A pretty girl in a fur coat, carrying a leather handbag, stood admiring a platinum bracelet in the window of a jewelry store.
10. After a few moments of deathly silence, the east wind brought us the sound of their birdlike chatter.
11. She has the face of an angel and the figure of a temptress—but oh! what a scatterbrain!
12. I am planning to set out on an expedition before the end of November; as an archaeologist, I must study the ruins of Minos on the spot.
13. Not all cities on seven hills can be Rome: as concerns location, and opportunities as well, the City of Seven Hills stands alone.
14. Ever an ardent patriot, there was something of the charlatan and the circus barker in his manner.
15. In the middle of February, in the heart of the Rockies, I would expect more snow, but as a weather prophet I fear that I am not very good.
16. To enjoy the Alps with their white needles, you need the eye of an artist and the physique of a well-trained athlete.
17. On a small gas stove he heated some onion soup and made a mushroom omelette for his dinner.
18. The south wind brought sunny, springlike weather.
19. At the costume party he fell in love with a pretty red-haired stranger dressed as a shepherdess.
20. How lucky he was to be right on the spot while such stirring events were taking place!
21. As a reporter she is a great success; she is a young woman with a penetrating mind and a ready tongue.
22. The dining room has a French window that leads out into the vegetable garden; in the other rooms there are only sash windows.
23. An elementary school teacher, she earns around eighteen thousand dollars a year; her husband, an engineer, earns about forty thousand.
24. The study of law is not an easy task.
25. A mermaid is a mythical creature having the head of a woman and the tail of a fish.
26. Madame Danilova, the famous ballerina, had something of the goddess about her.
27. Those china teacups are really and truly fragile!*
28. At the end of May, we left for Venice, the city of canals and gondolas.
29. She would like to attend the concert—if there is a concert.
30. On the appointed day, he walked across fields and meadows to the cherry orchard to meet the beautiful stranger with violet eyes.

B. Sur une feuille séparée, traduire ce passage en tenant compte autant que possible des techniques étudiées jusqu'à présent.

The wood upon the hearth was flaring cheerfully, and the water, what there was of it, was boiling. The two brass candlesticks bore their flaming ministers bravely, one on each side of the mirror. The big fourposter, with its patchwork quilt of faded blues and scarlets and its chintz hangings dimmed by age and laundering, had, against the pale, plastered walls, a dignified air as though of exiled royalty. Harriet, warm and powdered and free at last from the smell of soot, paused with the hair brush in her hand to wonder what was happening to Peter. She slipped across the chill dark of the dressing-room, opened the farther door, and listened. From somewhere far below came an ominous clank of iron, followed by a loud yelp and a burst of half-suffocating laughter.

"Poor darling!" said Harriet. . . .

She put out the bedroom candles. The sheets, worn thin by age, were of fine linen, and somewhere in the room there was a scent of lavender. . . . A branch broke and fell upon the hearth in a shower of sparks, and the tall shadows danced across the ceiling.

Dorothy L. Sayers, *Busman's Honeymoon*
(New York: Harper & Row Perennial Mystery Library Series, 1967), pp. 57–58.

6 | LE PRONOM

Assimilation des structures

---

44 | EMPLOI DU PRONOM PERSONNEL *EN*

A. Traduire en employant *en* après *comme, tel que, autant que.*

Modèle: He showed us jewels the likes **of which** we had never seen in our lives.

- *Il nous a montré des bijoux comme nous n'**en** avions jamais vu de notre vie.*

---

1. He gave her a mink coat such as she had never dreamed of before.

2. Now I can afford to buy clothes the likes **of which** I have not ever possessed.

3. He has as many friends as any man could wish.

4. I have a headache the likes **of which** you could not possibly imagine.

5. They already have as many children as they can afford to support.

B. Traduire en employant *en* devant l'article indéfini + *autre.*

Modèle: He did not tell that story; it was another (**one**).

- *Il n'a pas raconté cette histoire-là; c'**en** était une autre.*

---

1. It wasn't that man who followed me, it was another (**one**).

2. This ticket is no longer valid; you will have to buy another.

3. The two o'clock bus has already left; there will be another **one** at two-thirty.

4. This napkin is soiled; please bring me another.

5. You may keep your pencil, I bought another **one.**

C. Traduire en employant *en* pléonastique pour mettre en relief le substantif qui suit.

Modèle: What a row there was, and the whole night long!

- *Il y **en** a eu du grabuge, et pendant toute la nuit!* *
  en + substantif

1. What a lot of coffee you drink!

2. There are a lot of women in my house!

3. He talks a lot of nonsense.

4. There are books galore in this room!

5. You do have nerve!

D. Traduire en employant *en* + l'article défini au lieu de l'adjectif possessif.

Modèle: She perceived **its** well-known spire.

- *Elle **en** aperçut **le** célèbre clocher.*

1. I was admiring **its** snowy slopes. (mountain)

2. The oceanographer is exploring **its** depths. (sea)

3. We are measuring **its** margin of error. (poll)

4. Without help, we will never reach **their** peaks. (mountains)

5. By removing everything that made the movie original, she was hoping to increase **its** marketability.

45 | PRONOMS DÉMONSTRATIFS *CECI* ET *CELA*

A. Traduire *this* ou *that* par l'adjectif démonstratif *ce* + un substantif précis, déterminé par le contexte.

that	contexte

Modèle: **That** is impossible. (*Il a refusé.*)

- *Ce **refus** est impossible.*
  ce + substantif
       précis

1. You had better drive carefully because of **that**. (*Il a neigé.*)

2. Their parents will never accept **that**. (*Roméo et Juliette veulent se marier.*)

3. **This** is ridiculous! (*Il n'est pas permis de fumer en classe.*)

4. She married him because of **that.** (*Son mari est très riche.*)

5. **This** looks delicious! (*On déjeune.*)

B. Traduire *this* ou *that* par une expression verbale précise, déterminée par le contexte.

---
that   contexte
Modèle: **That** is out of the question. (*Ils veulent partir avant l'heure convenue.*)
   ● *Il ne saurait être question de **partir avant l'heure convenue.***
                                               expression verbale précise
---

1. **This** is hard to believe. (*Une amie veut divorcer.*)

2. We have just heard about **that.** (*Pierre a eu un accident.*)

3. Do **this** at once or I'll spank you! (*L'enfant refuse de ramasser ses vêtements.*)

4. She wants **that** very much. (*Son père ne veut pas qu'elle continue ses études.*)

5. **That** makes me very happy! (*Ma meilleure amie s'est fiancée.*)

C. Traduire *it, this, that* par *cela* sujet neutre.

Modèle: They predicted rain for today, but happily **it** did not happen.
   ● *On a annoncé de la pluie pour aujourd'hui; heureusement **cela** ne s'est pas produit.*
---

1. She works very hard, but **it** is worth it.

2. We couldn't get tickets for tonight, but **it** makes no difference.

3. You don't need to explain your actions—**it**'s all right.

4. Marriage can strengthen love—**it** happens quite often.

5. Please come to our house for dinner; **it** would please us a lot.

*D. Traduire *he, she, him, her* par *ce* ou *ça* pour désigner une personne d'une façon péjorative.

Modèle: **She** is as ugly as homemade sin, and **she** thinks she is the queen of the neighborhood.
   ● *C'est laid comme une chenille et **ça** se croit la reine du quartier.*
---

1. **He** thinks he's so smart, and **he** makes one blunder after another.

2. Do you really intend to go out with **her?**

3. **She** simpers, **she** flirts, **she** flutters her eyelashes—**she** thinks she's so cute.

4. **He** is old, fat, and bald, and **he** thinks he is Don Juan!

5. Would any woman in her right mind marry **him?**

46 MOYENS DE PERMETTRE AU PRONOM RELATIF DE SUIVRE IMMÉDIATEMENT SON ANTÉCÉDENT

A. Traduire en employant l'inversion du sujet et du verbe afin que le pronom relatif se place immédiatement après son antécédent. (Traduire le participe présent, le cas échéant, par une proposition relative.)

Modèle: **People flocked** from all over just to see the traveling show.

- *De toutes parts **affluaient des gens qui** étaient venus rien que pour assister au théâtre ambulant.*
  verbe + sujet / antécédent + pronom relatif

1. **A man enters** asking to see the owner of the house.

2. **Two young women arrived,** insisting they had an appointment with the senator.

3. From all over the world **athletes came,** hoping to distinguish themselves in the Olympic Games.

4. Suddenly **acrobats appeared** onstage, turning somersaults.

5. Sometimes **events occur that** puzzle us.

B. Traduire en répétant l'antécédent immédiatement devant le pronom relatif.

Modèle: The professor outlined a panorama of the French novel, **which** was very useful to us.

antécédent / pronom relatif

- *Le professeur a esquissé un panorama du roman français, **panorama qui** nous a été fort utile.*
  antécédent répété + pronom relatif

1. Flaubert shows the mediocrity of provincial society in nineteenth-century France, **which** is stifling to Emma Bovary's romantic soul.

2. The museum presented an exhibition of the artist's late canvases, **which** were painted during his so-called Baltimore period.

3. We admired the stained-glass windows of Chartres Cathedral, **which** glowed with an extraordinary radiance of reds and blues.

4. In *The Flies,* Sartre uses the famous Greek legend of Electra and Orestes, **which** has inspired several other contemporary dramatists, notably Giraudoux and O'Neill.

5. Do not miss the Metropolitan Museum's exhibit of traditional costumes of all nations, **which** is on loan from museums in London, Paris, and Moscow.

C. Traduire en faisant précéder le pronom relatif d'un substantif en apposition qui précise ou résume un antécédent vague.

Modèle: The association is thinking of organizing tourist trips as soon as possible, (**an idea**) **which** displeases no one.

- *L'association pense organiser des voyages touristiques aussitôt que possible, **idée qui** ne déplaît à personne.*
  substantif en apposition + pronom relatif

1. Many tourists spend an inordinate amount of time taking photographs, **which (idiosyncrasy)** seems ridiculous to me.

2. A number of people drive while intoxicated, **which (imprudence)** is responsible for many accidents.

3. Our neighbors have just returned from a trip to the Soviet Union, **where** the state exercises absolute economic control.

4. She came home at midnight, **when** the streets are nearly deserted.

5. She quit her job and went back to school, **which (decision)** pleased her family and friends.

D. Traduire en employant *et qui, mais qui* ou *puis qui* pour lier une proposition relative à un antécédent modifié par une expression contenant un substantif.

Modèle: He is a world-renowned lawyer **who** is also a gifted and little-known poet.
- *C'est un avocat célèbre dans le monde entier, **mais qui** est aussi un poète doué et peu connu.*
  antécédent + substantif + pronom relatif

---

1. My cousin, a well-known film director **who** is also an incurable ladies' man, has just got married for the fifth time.

2. The new school in our neighborhood, **which** they began to build two years ago, is not yet completed.

3. Blaise Pascal, an eminent seventeenth-century philosopher **who** was a mathematician and a physicist as well, sought to prove the truth and excellence of the Christian religion.

4. Sir Winston Churchill, a statesman **who** was a serious painter too, had a worldwide reputation.

5. We bought a sofa, upholstered in pearl-gray mohair, **that** can be converted into a bed.

E. Traduire en employant *et qui, et que* ou *et dont* pour lier la proposition relative à son antécédent.

Modèle: He was an eccentric being **whose** presence amused many people.
- *C'était un être original **et dont** la présence amusait beaucoup de gens.*
  antécédent + pronom relatif

---

1. She is a great writer **whose** work is certain to survive.

2. They were mere charlatans **who** were never recognized by the scientists of their times.

3. This is an extremely serious accusation **that** should not be made lightly.

4. They will serve lavish refreshments, **which** will be supplied by the city's most elegant caterer.

5. He is a man-about-town **whose** life consists of a succession of meaningless social engagements.

F. Traduire en employant un verbe impersonnel pour permettre au pronom relatif de suivre immédiatement son antécédent.

Modèle: An opportunity presented itself from **which** we could all benefit.

- *Il s'est présenté une occasion que nous avons tous eu intérêt à saisir.*

$$\underset{\text{impersonnel}}{\text{verbe}} + \text{antécédent} + \underset{\text{relatif}}{\text{pronom}}$$

1. **An event occurred that** aroused great speculation and comment.

2. **A** curious **story comes back to me, which** my grandmother told me when I was very young.

3. **A** torrential **rain is falling that** could flood the entire area.

4. **A** mysterious **stranger came who** bore an urgent message.

5. After dinner, **only** a few **scraps remained, which** the dog swallowed in one mouthful.

G. Traduire en utilisant *celui, celle,* etc. pour permettre au pronom relatif de suivre immédiatement son antécédent.

Modèle: In Paris it was announced that Julien Green, the great American and French **writer** of novels and plays, has been elected to the French Academy.

- *À Paris, on annonce l'élection à l'Académie française de Julien Green, le grand **écrivain** américain et français, **celui qui** est l'auteur de romans et de pièces.*

1. We have recently met the big **industrialist** and notorious **playboy,** George Ducros, **who** is said to be irresistible to women.

2. She is reading an article about Lara Vallina, an American film **star** of the 1920s, **who** was known as "the Flame."

3. Allow me to introduce Joseph Lenoir, the **ski champion** and fearless **aviator who** holds the world's record for stunt flying.

4. He is writing his thesis on François Rabelais, a great **writer** of the French Renaissance, **who** wrote *Gargantua* and *Pantagruel.*

5. I am a true admirer of Dr. Jonas Salk, the world-famous **scientist** and **researcher who** discovered the polio vaccine.

H. Traduire en employant *c'est à qui, c'était à qui* ou *à qui mieux mieux.*

Modèle: They are vying with one another as to who will shout the loudest.

- *C'est à qui criera le plus fort.*

1. **They were vying as to who** would speak first.

2. **They are vying with each other as to who** will jump higher.

3. **They were vying as to who** would run the fastest.

4. **They are vying with one another as to who** will lift the heaviest weight.

5. **They were vying as to who** would drink the most.

47 | MOYENS D'ÉVITER LA MULTIPLICATION DE PROPOSITIONS RELATIVES

A. Remplacer la proposition relative par un substantif en apposition.

---

proposition relative

Modèle: Le Concorde, *qui représente un progrès important de la technologie moderne,* coûte cependant très cher au passager.

- *Le Concorde, **merveille** de la technologie moderne, coûte cependant très cher au passager.*
  substantif
  en apposition

---

1. Mon collègue, *qui enseigne l'anglais au lycée de Bourville,* fera une conférence sur la poésie de Wordsworth.

2. André Dionne, *qui a écrit cette poésie,* est un jeune poète d'avenir.

3. La statue de « La Liberté éclairant le monde, » *qui représente l'indépendance américaine,* fut le cadeau du peuple français.

4. La soprano Régine Crespin, *qui chantait à l'Opéra de Paris,* passait ses vacances en Grèce.

5. Cette jeune Américaine, *qui reçoit une bourse du gouvernement québécois,* fait des recherches sur Réjean Ducharme.

B. Traduire la proposition relative par un substantif.

---

proposition relative

Modèle: You have just heard **what is perfect in music.**

- *Vous venez d'entendre la **perfection musicale.***
  substantif

---

1. I cannot understand **what they are saying.**

2. **What we do** is more important than **what we feel.**

3. He loves to show off **what he knows.**

4. He could not foresee **what would happen as a result** of his thoughtlessness.

5. Everything **that Sartre wrote** bears a relation to his existentialist philosophy.

C. Traduire les mots en caractères gras d'abord par une proposition relative, et ensuite par un adjectif (y compris le participe employé comme adjectif) qui remplace cette proposition.

Modèle: All we see is young people **wearing** jeans.
- *Nous ne voyons que des jeunes **qui portent** des jeans.*
- *Nous ne voyons que des jeunes **vêtus de** jeans.*

---

1. The portly matron was followed by a meek little husband **carrying** a load of boxes and parcels.

2. They dwell in a minuscule village **nestled** in the heart of the Alps.

3. We drank from huge crystal goblets **brimful of** champagne.

4. She looked up at him with **mischievous** eyes.

5. **Equipped with** tents, sleeping bags, and food, the campers set out toward the woods.

D. Remplacer la proposition relative par un adjectif.

---

proposition relative

Modèle: Ce sont des aliments *que l'on peut à peine manger.*
- *Ce sont des aliments **à peine mangeables.***

adjectif

---

1. C'est de l'eau *que l'on peut boire.*

2. Ma sœur, *qui voit tout en rose,* est persuadée qu'elle a bien réussi à ses examens.

3. Notre voisin, *qui ne croit pas en Dieu,* continue à aller à la messe par tradition.

4. On exerce sur lui une pression *qu'il peut difficilement supporter.*

5. Il a l'air de cacher un secret *dont il a honte.*

E. Traduire et raccourcir l'énoncé en remplaçant la proposition relative par une préposition + pronom personnel tonique + participe ou adjectif.

---

proposition
relative

Modèle: At the ball I saw no one **whom I knew.**

- *Arrivé au bal, je n'ai vu personne **de moi connu***

préposition
+ pronom tonique
+ adjectif ou participe

---

1. What has he done with the documents **that were entrusted to him?**

2. Your friend has committed an act **that I cannot understand.**

3. She returned to her publishers the five chapters **that she had revised and corrected.**

4. They never acknowledged receipt of the five chapters **that were sent to them.**

5. In this little village, we never see anyone **whom we do not know.**

F. Traduire la proposition relative par une préposition + substantif.

---

proposition   relative
Modèle: He is a child **who is** constantly **fighting** his parents.

- *C'est un enfant **en lutte** constante avec ses parents.*
  préposition + substantif

---

1. He is a man **who is searching** for a better way of life.

2. My eldest sister, **who is unlike** other girls of her age, cares only for astrophysics and mountain climbing.

3. My grandfather, **who is the opposite** of his wife, thrives on attending concerts and the theater.

4. She is a fine secretary **who hopes** to enter a more lucrative field by studying computer programming.

5. Rabelais's books were condemned as heretical by the king, **who agreed** with the theologians of the Sorbonne.

Exercices de sélection

Pour tous ces exercices, discuter et comparer vos choix.
A. (44, 45)   Traduire les mots en caractères gras de deux façons différentes.

Modèle: He did not tell that story; it was another (**one**).

- *Il n'a pas raconté cette histoire-là; c'**en** était une autre.*
- *Il n'a pas raconté cette histoire-là; c'était une autre **histoire**.*

---

1. If you miss the seven o'clock flight, there is another (**one**) at eight.

2. This steak is too well done; bring me another (**one**).

3. He has **a lot of** nerve!*

4. **What** marvels she is accomplishing!

5. **That** surprises me. (*Il se conduit mal.*)

6. Don't worry about it; **it**'s not important.

7. **He** is silly and ignorant, and **he** thinks he knows it all.*

8. Why would such a lovely girl want to date **him?***

9. Look at all those cars crawling along at a snail's pace; because of **that,** we are going to be late.

10. He tried to pass the examination by cheating, but **it** didn't work.

B. (46, 47) Traduire les mots en caractères gras par au moins deux constructions différentes.

Modèle: Our guide, **who** already **knew** the language of the country, managed really well.

- *Notre guide se débrouillait formidablement bien, **lui qui connaissait** déjà la langue du pays.* *
- *Notre guide se débrouillait formidablement bien, **connaissant** déjà la langue du pays.* *
- *Notre guide se débrouillait formidablement bien, la langue du pays **lui** étant déjà **familière**.* *
- *Il se débrouillait formidablement bien, notre guide **qui connaissait** déjà la langue du pays.* *

---

1. Sometimes **events occur that** take us by surprise.

2. On the beaches of the Mediterranean, one meets young people of all nations, **wearing** jeans and **carrying** sleeping bags.

3. I have just read a book about the Middle Ages, **when** the Catholic Church had an enormous influence on every aspect of French culture.

4. He found his wife asleep on the chair, still **holding** a lighted cigarette between her fingers.

5. Many individuals in the Western world, **seeking** inner peace, have embraced Eastern religions.

6. There is a man **whom people admire.**

7. Numerous colleges encourage students to study abroad, **which enables** Americans to acquire fluency in foreign languages.

8. She fails to realize **what will happen as a result of** her impulsive act.

9. Suddenly **a face** I had not seen for years **appeared** before my eyes.

10. This adolescent, **who has written** two plays and several volumes of poetry, is already hailed as an important writer of the new generation.

Exercices de synthèse

A. Sur une feuille séparée, traduire les phrases suivantes en utilisant les techniques suggérées dans le chapitre consacré au pronom.

1. Here is one such as you often see in shop windows, but you will not get another like the one you lost.

2. That is not easy to achieve, but this much is certain: She will keep on trying, and I admire that very much.
3. I heard lots of praise for that singer, to which was added some regret for the brevity of her programs.
4. What a silly girl! She primps, she preens, she admires herself in the mirror—she thinks she's one of the seven wonders of the world.*
5. In preparing this exercise, you may use both grammar books and dictionaries, which tools are practically indispensable.
6. The boys vied with each other picking apples. [*plus d'une façon*]
7. I prefer this statue, which is wearing a halo, to that one, which is bereft of such an ornament.
8. Congress will assemble on Thursday, March 20, when it will take up the committee's report on the president's proposal to aid the unemployed.
9. He is a charming, naturally modest man who does not easily take offense.
10. The sky, which formerly symbolized infinity, has dwindled into mere "space," to be explored and conquered.
11. Julien, who was fundamentally in conflict with the society in which he lived, sought to conceal his true convictions beneath a mask of hypocrisy.
12. This is a situation with which she is perfectly capable of dealing, I am certain of that.
13. What a lot of fuss he made—but it was worth it!
14. She got a sunburn the likes of which I have never seen in my life!
15. You had better take care of the body you have, for you will never get another.
16. We attended a Breton folk-dance festival that was held last July just outside Quimper.
17. Haig is a cellist of international fame who is also an avid pianist.
18. Last summer they revisited Lake Como, where they had first met.
19. The lecturer poured forth a torrent of verbiage that we could not understand.
20. She is a celebrated wit whose caustic sallies have offended many people.
21. At the embassy reception, I did not meet a single person I knew.
22. The doctor has been delayed by an emergency; because of that, all his appointments must be rescheduled.
23. What a lot of writers she knows—talented ones, whose work is famous all over the world.
24. The ballet represents what is most refined in the art of dance.
25. We know a colleague who is eternally at war with her environment.
26. The museums of Florence are filled with as many priceless treasures as it is possible to imagine.
27. My office mate was a confirmed optimist, who always expected the best of everyone.
28. Let's not go into the city today; it isn't worth the trouble.
29. Gilbert, who plays the leading role in the drama, gave a superb performance.
30. They served us a dinner that was virtually inedible.

B. Sur une feuille séparée, traduire ce passage en tenant compte autant que possible des techniques étudiées jusqu'à présent.

> Miranda looked from one to the other of them understandingly, and sat down. She was wearing a négligée that strictly belonged to her trousseau, pale blue velvet; its long wide skirts dropped in graceful folds, beneath which the toe of a pale blue mule peeped provocatively forth. . . .
> "Dadda, Harry!" she cried gaily. "What a fuss! Whatever Harry wants to tell I want to hear! Did you kiss her good-by, Harry, after all? If you did, I'm not jealous! How could I be," laughed Miranda, "of such a scarecrow?"
> As Mr. Joyce subsequently remarked, in one of his new slangy phrases, that tore it.
> For a moment, Harry didn't comprehend; then the blood rushed up to his face, and all his love, even his fury, burst forth in one outraged cry.
> "How dare you!" roared Harry Gibson. "Not jealous! What else but jealousy is that lie?"
> Miranda instantly jumped up. If he was furious, so now was she.

"What lie? Calling that creature a scarecrow?" She laughed again, but on a very different note. "Let me tell you, Dadda called her far worse! A skeleton, a bag of bones—"

"Miranda, for God's sake!" implored Mr. Joyce.

"—a Kiss of Death!" finished Miranda recklessly. "And I say so too!"

"Keep your tongue off her!" shouted Harry Gibson. "Now *I'*ll tell *you* something!"

"Stop!" shouted Mr. Joyce. "He's mad!" he added rapidly to Miranda. "Don't listen to him! Go to bed! Leave it to me."

"I'm going to marry her," said Harry Gibson, suddenly calm. . . . "That's right: I'm jilting you."

Miranda turned. There was no love in her eyes. There was still incredulity—but of a new sort. She had seen Miss Diver twice, and once no doubt at her smartest. . . .

"For *that* thing?"*

"For the lady whose name is Miss Diver," returned Harry dangerously. "Yes."

Margery Sharp, *The Eye of Love*
(Boston: Little, Brown, 1957), pp. 255–258.

7 | LA PRÉPOSITION

Assimilation des structures

48 | AMPLIFICATION EN FRANÇAIS DE LA SIMPLE PRÉPOSITION ANGLAISE

A. Traduire en remplaçant la simple préposition par une préposition + infinitif.

Modèle: We know his yearning **for** fame.
- *Nous connaissons son désir **de devenir** célèbre.*
  préposition
  + infinitif

1. I could never tire **of** my job.

2. She is not afraid **of** his anger.

3. He was delighted **by** her recovery.

4. She was amazed **at** her own serenity.

5. He was disconcerted **by** my frankness.

B. Traduire en remplaçant la simple préposition par *en* + participe présent (c.-à-d. le gérondif).

Modèle: The women can continue their discussion **over** dinner.
- *Les femmes peuvent continuer leur discussion tout **en prenant** leur repas.*
  en + participe présent (= gérondif)

1. **In** view of the facts, the actress took on new kinds of roles.

2. **With** a shrug of the shoulders, he dismissed the unwelcome suspicion from his mind.

3. She will take the test over **in** the hope of earning a better grade.

4. "Be quiet!" he commanded **with** a frown.

5. We settled the matter amicably **over** drinks.

C. Traduire en ajoutant devant la préposition un participe passé qui spécifie l'action.

Modèle: The mouse observes the cat **on** the windowsill.

- *La souris regarde le chat **étiré sur** le rebord de la fenêtre.*

$$\frac{\text{participe}}{\text{passé}} + \text{préposition}$$

1. **In** his favorite armchair, he relaxes and watches television.

2. **With** a sable coat, a woman need no longer fear the cold.

3. One should never consider criticism as an attack **on** one's integrity.

4. **In** his arms, she forgot all her cares.

5. The feud **between** the two families is at an end.

D. Traduire la simple préposition par une locution prépositive (préposition + substantif + préposition).

Modèle: **For** chairs, people used boxes.

- ***En guise de** chaises on s'est servi de caisses.*
  préposition
  + substantif
  + préposition

1. Attention! Flight 70 **from** London **to** Rome is now arriving at gate 10.

2. I am writing an article **about** existentialism.

3. Untold treasures lay buried **within** the hold of the sunken ship.

4. He was praised **for** his scientific discoveries.

5. We have greetings for you **from** your friends in Boston.

E. Traduire en ajoutant devant la préposition une proposition relative qui spécifie l'action.

Modèle: The friendship **between** us will pass every test.

- *L'amitié **qui existe entre** nous résistera à toutes les épreuves.*
  proposition + préposition
  relative

1. The French language contains a great many words **from** Greek and Latin.

2. Listen to the rain **against** the windowpanes!

3. I know of certain means **toward** greater self-awareness.

4. There is a tiny brook **behind** the house.

5. We could hear a gentle breeze **among** the branches.

F. Traduire en ajoutant un adjectif devant la préposition.

Modèle: **With** his willpower, the student was able to pass the examination.

- *Fort de sa volonté, l'étudiant a pu réussir à l'examen.*
  adjectif
  + préposition

1. **Beneath** her makeup she seemed rather tired.

2. **On** a leafy branch, a solitary bird was singing.

3. **In** her mink cape, she strode jauntily along **in** the icy wind.

4. **On** his black horse, he drew all eyes.

5. **With** her magnificent crown, she looked like a queen.

G. Traduire en remplaçant la préposition par une tournure verbale.

Modèle: The cashier will return **for** her belongings around eight o'clock.

- *La caissière repassera **prendre** ses affaires vers huit heures.*
       tournure
       verbale

1. Go **for** a doctor at once!

2. Critics hailed the work as a great novel **with** severe weaknesses.

3. I will come **for** you right after dinner.

4. He is going to visit the home **of** his early childhood.

5. She must go **to** him right away.

H. Remplacer le complément introduit par une préposition par un substantif sujet de la phrase.

préposition + substantif
Modèle: *Par sa pérséverance elle obtint de l'avancement.*

- *Sa persévérance lui valut un avancement.*
       substantif sujet

1. Il y a un superbe jardin baroque *derrière la haie.*

2. *Dans ce tiroir* il y a des chemises et des caleçons.

3. *À cause de ce mariage* elle est maintenant richissime.*

4. Il y avait un excellent cidre *à l'intérieur du gobelet.*

5. Elle devint célèbre *grâce à son premier roman.*

I. Traduire les deux constructions prépositives en remplaçant le substantif de la seconde par un pronom.

---

préposition 1 + préposition 2 + substantif

Modèle: Our senator is **generous toward** and **loved by** the people.

● *Notre sénateur se montre **généreux envers** le peuple et il **en** est **aimé.***

préposition 1 + substantif + pronom

---

1. Your friends are **aware of** and **grateful for** your kindness.

2. The union members have been **apprised of,** and are strongly **opposed to,** the proposed contract.

3. His parents are **delighted by** and **proud of** his progress.

4. She is **in charge of** and fully **responsible for** the new program.

5. Many women are rigidly **circumscribed by,** and heartily **weary of,** their family responsibilities.

49 | PRÉPOSITIONS: REMARQUES DIVERSES

A. Traduire en intercalant une courte locution entre *avec* et son complément.

---

compléments   +   locution

Modèle: There is the property, with ponds and gardens **here and there.**

● *Voilà la propriété avec, **par-ci par-là,** des étangs et des jardins.*

locution   +   compléments

---

1. The painting represented a cottage with rosebushes and shrubs **all around it.**

2. The sky was a flat expanse of pale blue with one or two hazy white clouds **in the far distance.**

3. He listened to her words with infinite tenderness **in his heart.**

4. All we could see was dull blue waves with foamy crests **now and then.**

5. She looked at him with a surge of **involuntary** attraction.

*B. Traduire en terminant la phrase par une préposition.

---

préposition + pronom

Modèle: The boy snatches the cat to play **with it.**

● *Le garçon attrape le chat pour jouer **avec.***

préposition

---

1. She ordered steak tartare with an egg **on top** and onions **around it.**

2. I see the table, but I can't tell what the object **under it** is.

3. Overcome by dizziness, she staggered to the door and leaned **against it.**

4. He peered into his wallet and found nothing **in it.**

5. When we arrived at the hotel, our guide was waiting for us **in front of it.**

C. Traduire en employant les prépositions *d'avec* ou *contre*. Dire si la préposition dénote la séparation ou l'échange.

---

préposition

Modèle: This store sells its products **for** cash only.

- *Ce magasin ne vend ses produits que **contre** espèces.*

préposition
(dénote échange)

---

1. It is not easy to distinguish true love **from** infatuation.

2. I wish I could exchange this magnificent diamond **for** a simple gold band.

3. This is the test that separates the strong **from** the weak.

4. It is virtually impossible to tell an authentic Paris Cartier watch **from** a fake Mexican reproduction.

5. She wouldn't trade her one old, faithful husband **for** two sexy young lovers!

D. Traduire en employant la préposition *moyennant*. Dire si la préposition dénote l'échange, le moyen ou le résultat.

---

préposition

Modèle: The store provides home delivery **on** payment of ten francs.

- *Le magasin livre à domicile **moyennant** paiement de dix francs.*

préposition
(dénote échange)

---

1. **For** one thousand dollars, plus monthly payments, you can own this elegant red convertible.

2. **By means of** a sensible, moderate diet she can lose twenty pounds in two months.

3. Politicians, **in exchange for** certain favors, will lobby on behalf of particular interest groups.

4. They deduct seventy-five dollars a week from his salary, **in return for** which he receives, every ten weeks, a one thousand-dollar bond.

5. I hope to remain in good health **thanks to** a few simple precautions.

E. Traduire *from* et *out of* par la préposition *dans*.

Modèle: We drink hot chocolate **from** a bowl.

- *Nous buvons du chocolat **dans** un bol.*

1. He took a cigarette **from** his pocket.

2. She is taking a notebook and a pencil **out of** her handbag.

3. The artist sculpted a giant eagle **out of** bronze.

4. She has a scrapbook of recipes cut **from** newspapers.

5. The child grabbed a cookie **from** the jar and gobbled it up.

F. En traduisant la préposition, choisir entre *à, en* et *dans*. Justifier votre choix.

Modèle: We live **in** Lyon, but not **in** Lyon proper.

- *Nous habitons **à** Lyon, mais pas **dans** Lyon.*

  Justification: *dans,* plus spécifique, traduit la nuance de sens qui distingue *Lyon proper* de *Lyon* tout court.

1. The carpenter is holding a hammer **in** his hand.

2. My mother is **at** home.

3. She is **inside** the house.

4. **In** modern Greece, many classical traditions are preserved.

5. They spent their vacation **in** Spain.

G. En traduisant la préposition, choisir entre *dans, sur* et *à même*.

Modèle: He was drinking **right out of** the bottle.

- *Il buvait **à même** la bouteille.*

1. A table and two chairs stood **on** the sidewalk in front of the small café.

2. **On** every windowsill the decorator placed a planter box of ivy.

3. They lay down **on** the floor **itself.**

4. I saw a soldier drinking **right from** the water bottle.

5. In Poland they drink tea **from** a glass.

H. Traduire en employant correctement la préposition *de.*

Modèle: The swimming pool is eight meters **long.**
- *La piscine fait huit mètres **de long.***

1. His mistress is **five years older than** he.

2. She is **considerably** more intelligent than he.

3. The classroom is fifteen meters **long** and twelve meters **wide.**

4. I have never **in my life** met anyone like him.

5. We will not see the Paris Opera in New York again **for a long time.**

I. Traduire en employant *de* pour indiquer le passage d'un état à l'autre.

Modèle: He suddenly changed **from** an adolescent to a mature man.
- ***D**'adolescent il devint soudain homme mûr.*

1. She changed **from** an ugly duckling to a singularly beautiful swan.

2. Lagneau changed **from** a dunce to a top-rate student.*

3. The summer slipped away, and the work, **previously** a joy, became sheer drudgery.

4. At the end, the figure in the portrait metamorphosed **from** a fresh, handsome youth to a corrupt, loathsome old man.

5. After only one year of marriage, she changed **from** a slim, attractive girl to a plump, sober matron.

J. En traduisant, choisir entre *durant, en, par* et *à.*

Modèle: He worked **throughout** his entire life.
- *Il travailla sa vie **durant.***

1. The lights went out **one by one.**

2. She ran downstairs **three steps at a time.**

3. They adored each other **for** fifteen years.

4. You should never believe the things he says; they are only **cock-and-bull stories.**

5. They spoke **for** hours **on end.**

K. En traduisant, choisir entre *en, par* et *à*.

Modèle: It took courage to venture forth **in** such weather!

- *Il a fallu du courage pour sortir **par** un temps pareil!*

1. They gave a formal dinner **in** his honor.

2. **In** their parents' absence, the children turned the whole house upside down.

3. **On** a gloomy night, a lonely figure rode over to the parsonage.

4. The animals boarded the ark two **by** two.

5. She deserves a really lavish gift—**under** the circumstances, a diamond bracelet.

L. En traduisant, choisir entre *par, pour* et *envers*.

Modèle: **To** a great artist, the whole world is a source of inspiration.

- ***Pour** un grand artiste, le monde entier est source d'inspiration.*

1. Leblanc, the eminent author, is famous **for** his eccentricity.

2. Her older sister is extremely kind **to** her.

3. They are going away on vacation **for** three weeks.

4. The countess is renowned **for** her elegance as well as **for** her extravagance.

5. The world seems gloriously, radiantly lovely **on** a dazzling summer afternoon.

M. Traduire en employant correctement les prépositions *à . . . près* et *sans*.

Modèle: Certain cubist paintings resemble one another, **with the exception of form and nuances.**

- *Certaines peintures cubistes se ressemblent, **à la forme et aux nuances près.***

1. We studied the works of all the English romantic poets, **with one or two exceptions.**

2. **Were it not for** her work, she would move to the country.

3. **But for** the unending rain and fog, Seattle would be an ideal home city.

4. The copy resembles the original, **with precious little difference.**

5. **Had it not been for** her courage and presence of mind, her entire family would have perished in the fire.

N. Traduire en employant correctement les locutions prépositives *à la suite de* et *par suite de*.

Modèle: They are **in pursuit of** a robber.

- *Ils sont **à la suite** d'un voleur.*

1. Three respectful assistants and one adoring secretary walked **in the wake of** the great man.

2. **Because of** a computer error, he continued to be billed for several months after he had paid in full.

3. **In view of** the urgency of the situation, a special meeting was called.

4. She received a substantial increase in salary **following** her promotion.

5. **As a result of** a chill, she caught a severe case of pneumonia.

O. Traduire en employant correctement les prépositions *sur* et *contre*.

Modèle: The director was questioned **about** his motives.

● *On a interrogé le directeur **sur** ses motifs.*

1. She is the author of several fine books **on** the French surrealists.

2. He arrived **about** six o'clock.

3. A single rosy streak stands out **against** the darkening sky.

4. Oaks and fir trees rise **against** the mountainside.

5. Two dark silhouettes were etched **against** a white background.

P. Traduire en employant *étant donné* soit avant, soit après le substantif, et faire l'accord nécessaire.

Modèle: **Given** the enormous wealth at his disposal, he is now in a position to help his family.

● ***Étant donné** les immenses richesses dont il dispose, il est maintenant à même d'aider les siens.*

Modèle: **In view of** the circumstances, it is imperative that those responsible do their duty.

● *Ces circonstances **étant données,** il importe que les responsables s'acquittent de leur devoir.*

1. I think they have done superb work, **considering** the obstacles.

2. **In view of** the defendant's extreme youth, the court took a lenient stance in its decision.

3. **Taking into account** the pressures to which he was subjected, it is remarkable that he was able to create so substantial a body of work.

4. **Given** the new evidence, the counsel for the defense moved for a brief recess.

5. **Considering** the deep-rooted prejudices prevalent in society, I sometimes wonder if we will ever achieve true equality.

Exercices de sélection

Pour tous ces exercices, discuter et comparer vos choix.

A. (48) Traduire la préposition par au moins deux constructions différentes.

Modèle: The mouse observes the cat **on** the windowsill.
- *La souris regarde le chat **étiré sur** le rebord de la fenêtre.*
- *La souris regarde le chat **qui reste étendu sur** le rebord de la fenêtre.*
- *La souris regarde le chat **à plat ventre sur** le rebord de la fenêtre.*
- *La souris regarde le chat **immobile sur** le rebord de la fenêtre.*

---

1. "You'll see!" he said **with a wink.**

2. **With a slingshot,** David vanquished the mighty Goliath.

3. She is ranked **among** the foremost artists of our generation.

4. They thought she was **at death's door,** but she astounded them by making a rapid recovery.

5. He will come **for** me **about** seven o'clock.

6. **As a result of that brilliant idea,** he was promoted.

7. The smoke **in** that room made me choke.

8. We can discuss the problem at length **over** coffee.

9. The misunderstanding **between** them was soon cleared up.

10. You must be aware of **his dread of** spiders.

B. (48, 49) Traduire les mots en caractères gras d'au moins deux façons.

Modèle: The soldiers were forced to stretch out **on** the ground **itself.**
- *Les soldats ont dû s'allonger **à même** le sol.*
- *Les soldats ont dû s'allonger **sur** le sol **même.***
- *Les soldats ont dû s'allonger **au niveau du** sol.*
- *Les soldats ont dû s'allonger **au ras du** sol.*

---

1. They drank **straight from** the bottle.

2. She **is about to leave.**

3. He has always been loving **toward** me.

4. He wrote his thesis **on** the Pre-Raphaelites.

5. Our living room is seven meters **long** and five meters **wide.**

6. **By means of** a few simple daily exercises, she has remained healthy and active up to the age of ninety-seven!

7. That minister is **considerably** more able than his predecessor.

8. He is determined to live **in** the city.

9. The genius of this painter has been recognized **for some time.**

10. **For** eleven years she labored to create her masterpiece.

Exercices de synthèse

A. Sur une feuille séparée, traduire les phrases suivantes en utilisant les techniques suggérées dans le chapitre consacré à la préposition.

1. All week long I could not find a free moment.
2. A broad-shouldered man with a tall silk hat paced the floor for hours.
3. This story is copied out of Proust's novel *Du côté de chez Swann.*
4. I asked her who was the wiser, her sister or herself.
5. You must distinguish a limited from a constitutional monarchy.
6. How dear to my heart are the scenes of my childhood.
7. All these ambitions are nothing compared with your happiness.
8. Ever since that difference of opinion between us, I have had no influence on her.
9. We were astonished by her sudden appearance; with a laugh, she greeted us warmly.
10. On a stifling hot night, I found him on the bed; his arms were stretched out across the pillow.
11. A letter from the treasurer for the president was lost in the mail.
12. In the absence of the dean, the toast will be drunk in honor of the university senators.
13. Franklin walked the length of Broad Street in coarse boots and with a loaf of bread under each arm.
14. Every time I threw the ball, the dog ran after it; this game went on for two hours—the dog was far more energetic than I was.*
15. Let me go for it; it will be appreciated by and valuable to all of them.
16. "How much younger are you than he?" "Not much, but he is by far the strongest in the class."
17. These days, farmers are bartering their wheat for cattle.
18. She ran upstairs three steps at a time; for a woman of forty, she is in excellent shape.*
19. Whether from friendship or from self-interest, he was very kind to me.
20. This movie star has been divorced from her husband for five years already.
21. Except for a few corrections, the work was absolutely perfect, considering the conditions she worked under.
22. His tall figure was silhouetted against the brilliant background.
23. As a result of this activity, I would have succeeded, had it not been for the interference of that meddler.
24. In my opinion, she is far superior to all other so-called child prodigies, with only one exception.
25. She was impressed by his responsiveness to the feelings of others.
26. If it were not for his lack of discipline, he could be one of the most important writers of our time.
27. In one summer she changed from a sulky child to a charming young woman.
28. With a yawn, the passenger across from me took a sandwich and a bottle of wine from his knapsack and proceeded to drink right out of the bottle.

29. I know a man who pursued success for fifteen years; then when he had achieved it, he found he couldn't live with it.*
30. Although she was renowned for her wealth, she would have exchanged it for a youthful, healthy body.

B. Sur une feuille séparée, traduire ce passage en tenant compte autant que possible des techniques étudiées jusqu'à présent.

Ransom himself could only describe it by saying that for his first few days in Perelandra he was haunted, not by a feeling of guilt, but by surprise that he had no such feeling. There was an exuberance or prodigality of sweetness about the mere act of living which our race finds it difficult not to associate with forbidden and extravagant actions. Yet it is a violent world too. Hardly had he lost sight of the floating object when his eyes were stabbed by an unendurable light. A grading, blue-to-violet illumination made the golden sky seem dark by comparison and in a moment of time revealed more of the new planet than he had yet seen. He saw the waste of waves spread illimitably before him, and far away, at the very end of the world, against the sky, a single smooth column of ghastly green standing up, the one thing fixed and vertical in this universe of shifting slopes. Then the rich twilight rushed back (now seeming almost darkness) and he heard thunder. But it has a different *timbre* from terrestrial thunder, more resonance, and even, when distant, a kind of tinkling. It is the laugh, rather than the roar, of heaven. Another flash followed, and another, and then the storm was all about him.

C. S. Lewis, *Perelandra*
(New York: Macmillan, 1968), p. 37.

8 | LA CONJONCTION

Assimilation des structures

50 | PROPOSITIONS SUBORDONNÉES

A. Remplacer la proposition subordonnée par un substantif.

Modèle: Le metteur en scène exige *que ses acteurs jouent* parfaitement.
- *Le metteur en scène exige **de ses acteurs un jeu** parfait.*
                                                    substantif

1. Nous regrettons *qu'il soit parti.*

2. Ils savent *que leur collègue est compétente.*

3. Elle craint *que son élève ne se fâche.*

4. Il exige *que ses étudiants travaillent* sérieusement.

5. Le dictateur veut *qu'on lui obéisse* totalement.

B. Traduire les mots en caractères gras d'abord par une proposition subordonnée, puis par un infinitif.

Modèle: Few writers fear **being considered** failures.
- Peu d'écrivains craignent *qu'on ne les considère comme* des ratés.*
- *Peu d'écrivains craignent **de passer pour** des ratés.*

1. All children enjoy **being given** gifts.

2. She insists on **being allowed** to make her own decisions.

3. We want **her to be** happy.

4. His parents saved for years **so that he could go** to college.

5. Now it is essential **that they start over** from the beginning.

C. Traduire la proposition par une proposition participe en construction absolue.

Modèle: When their research is finished, scholars feel greatly relieved.

- *Leur travail de recherche terminé, les savants éprouvent un grand soulagement.*
  proposition participe

1. **Once one goal has been attained,** we must find another to pursue.

2. **When his thesis was completed,** he applied for a position at a prestigious university.

3. **After their children have left home,** many couples begin a new life together.

4. **Once I had visited Quebec,** I decided to settle there permanently.

5. **Upon returning from Africa,** he began work on a new book.

D. Traduire la proposition par une forme impérative ou interrogative.

Modèle: If you go ahead with your project, it will pay off.

- *Poursuivez votre projet, ce sera une affaire qui rapportera.*
  forme impérative

1. **If you try,** you are sure to succeed.

2. **Why run away?** You cannot escape from yourself.

3. **If you make them laugh,** they will love you.

4. **Why bother to master tennis?** You're still not interested in it.

5. **If we have a little drink,** we will feel better.

51 | PROPOSITION SUBORDONNÉE COMPLÉMENT D'OBJET DIRECT

A. Éviter la proposition subordonnée en remplaçant le verbe d'opinion par une préposition + substantif.

$$\text{verbe d'opinion} + \text{proposition subordonnée}$$

Modèle: *Les psychiatres disent que* l'être humain est essentiellement stable.

- *D'après (Selon) le dire des psychiatres, l'être humain est essentiellement stable.*
  préposition + substantif

1. *Les professeurs estiment que* les fautes de grammaire sont inexcusables.

2. *L'enfant croit que* son père est digne d'admiration.

3. *Ma mère prétend que* les courants d'air sont extrêmement dangereux.

4. *Les critiques considèrent que* son dernier roman est nettement supérieur aux précédents.

5. *Certaines personnes imaginent que* l'on peut réussir sans travailler.

B. Traduire en remplaçant les deux verbes par un seul verbe.

---

verbe   +   verbe

Modèle: His brother **thinks that he is** a genius.

- *Son frère **le dit** génial.*

un verbe

---

1. His students **think he is** hard-hearted.

2. We **feel that he is** innocent.

3. Her teachers **believe she is** an excellent student.

4. Her parents **wish her to be** perfect.

5. His friends **consider that he is** a genius.

C. Traduire en remplaçant la proposition subordonnée par une tournure à l'infinitif.

Modèle: The mayor admits **that he did not consult** the city council.

- *Le maire admet **ne pas avoir consulté** le conseil municipal.*

infinitif

---

1. He thinks **that he knows** everything.

2. She insisted **that she was** right.

3. Many mothers claim **that they have sacrificed** their lives for their children.

4. We did not expect **that we would have to spend** so much money.

5. He believed **that he had lost** his willpower and initiative.

D. Traduire la proposition subordonnée selon le modèle suivant.

---

sujet + *être* + épithète

Modèle: I imagine **that Mauritius is glorious** with colors and fragrances.

- *J'imagine **l'île Maurice resplendissante** de couleurs et de parfums.*

objet direct   +   épithète

---

1. The critics believe **that this painter is exceptionally gifted.**

2. She thinks **that she is intelligent.**

3. They had imagined **that Tahiti was wild and romantic.**

4. Even his enemies said **that he was a hero.**

5. We thought **that she was more compassionate.**

E. Traduire la proposition subordonnée par une tournure comportant un objet indirect.

---

conjonction + sujet + verbe

Modèle: The people did not know **that she had** so many virtues.

- *Le peuple ne **lui** savait pas tant de vertus.*
      object
      indirect

---

1. I believed **that she was** a very charitable person.

2. I suspect **that this fellow has** expensive tastes.

3. She found **that he had** many good qualities.

4. We did not know **that they had** such strong convictions.

5. He fancied **that she had** infinite patience.

52 | PROPOSITION TEMPORELLE

A. Traduire la proposition temporelle par un participe passé.

Modèle: As soon as it was completed, the sonata assured its composer's renown.

- ***Aussitôt terminée,** la sonate fit la renommée de son compositeur.*
      participe passé

---

1. **As soon as he returned home,** he sat down in front of the television set.

2. **Once he was dead,** he became a legend.

3. **After it was published,** the novel enjoyed a unique success.

4. **The moment those words were spoken,** she regretted them.

5. **Just as soon as they were married,** they started a family.

B. Traduire la proposition temporelle par un substantif + participe passé ou par un pronom + participe.

Modèle: Once the preparations are over and done with, we will at last be able to leave on our trip.

- ***Les préparatifs terminés,** nous pourrons enfin partir en voyage.*
      substantif + participe

---

1. **Once the scandal had been forgotten,** he returned to his native land.

2. **After the artist died,** his paintings tripled in price.

3. **After signing the contract,** the author resumed work with renewed energy.

4. **After rehearsals had begun,** the playwright had little to do.

5. **Now that they have left,** we can forget the incident.

C. Traduire la proposition temporelle par une préposition + substantif.

Modèle: After peace had been declared, the nations showed their joy and happiness.

● *Après la déclaration de paix, les peuples manifestèrent leur joie et leur bonheur.*
préposition + substantif

---

1. I am anxious to return home **before night falls.**

2. **While the poem was being read,** the audience remained silent.

3. Please stay seated **until the class is over.**

4. **When the sun sets,** the horizon glows with fire.

5. **Because she was innately kind,** she had many friends.

D. Traduire la proposition temporelle par une préposition + infinitif.

Modèle: The lawyer decides to inquire into the case **before he defends** the accused.

● *L'avocat décide d'enquêter sur l'affaire **avant de défendre** l'accusé.*
préposition + infinitif

---

1. It is dangerous to drive **after you have been drinking.**

2. He had to write twelve hours a day **in order that he might finish** his manuscript before the deadline.

3. **As we were about to leave,** we had an unexpected visitor.

4. You must consider all aspects of the situation **before you make up your mind.**

5. **As he was on the point of committing himself** to the project, he became seriously ill.

E. Traduire la proposition temporelle par un participe présent ou un gérondif (*en* + participe présent).

Modèle: Breaking through a wall, the prisoner escapes unnoticed in the night.

● *Faisant une brèche dans un mur, le prisonnier s'évade inaperçu dans la nuit.*
participe présent

---

1. **As he was crossing the street,** he narrowly escaped being run over.

2. **Having completed her apprenticeship,** she is now eligible for professional stage roles.

3. It was **while he was watching a teakettle boil** that he first conceived the notion of the steamboat.

4. **Swallowing the last mouthful of his dinner,** he goes upstairs to study.

5. She hums softly to herself **while working.**

F. Traduire la proposition temporelle par un adjectif ou un substantif en apposition.

Modèle: The poor, **once they are liberated,** will at last be able to benefit from the public good.

   ● *Les pauvres, **libérés,** pourront enfin jouir du bien de la patrie.*
       adjectif
       (épithète
       détachée)

Modèle: Green, **when he was an old man,** wrote the most touching volume of his autobiography.

   ● *Green, **vieillard,** écrivit le tome le plus touchant de son autobiographie.*
       substantif
       en apposition

1. Marcel, **when he was a child,** was frightened of going to sleep.

2. The voters, **now that they have been disappointed,** no longer trust him.

3. **Every time she was embarrassed,** she would blush bright red.

4. **When she was a young girl,** she already bossed everybody.

5. **When he was a senator,** he introduced a number of reform bills.

53 PROPOSITION CONDITIONNELLE

A. Traduire la proposition conditionnelle par *à* + infinitif.

Modèle: **If you met him** by chance in the street, you would think him a friendless orphan.

   ● *À **le rencontrer** par hasard dans la rue, vous diriez un orphelin délaissé.*
     à + infinitif

1. **If you listened to her,** you would think she was the most talented poet of her generation.

2. **If they judged** by appearances, everyone would assume that he was a pauper.

3. **If you saw her,** you would think she was perfectly charming.

4. **If we** truly **knew them,** we would find them to be gentle, harmless people.

5. **If one accepted his version of creation,** one would be convinced of the existence of malevolent gods.

B. Traduire la proposition conditionnelle par *rien qu'à* + infinitif.

Modèle: If he suspects that there might be an insect present, the child jumps in fear.
- ● ***Rien qu'à soupçonner*** *la présence d'un insecte, l'enfant sursaute de peur.*
  rien qu'à + infinitif

---

1. **If I hear** an unexpected noise, I get goose bumps.

2. **If she even imagines** his voice, she yearns to hold him in her arms.

3. **By merely reading** the first chapter of her novel, one recognizes the flowering of a major talent.

4. **Just listening** to him speak, we experience a sense of calm and security.

5. **If she but suspects** that someone is criticizing her, she becomes that much more insecure.

C. Traduire la proposition conditionnelle en utilisant l'inversion.

Modèle: If she were to step forward as a candidate, she would be accepted.
- ● ***Se proposerait-elle*** *comme candidate, on l'accepterait.*
  inversion

---

1. **If he were to reveal** his identity, he would find himself in danger.

2. **If they had spoken,** they would have been listened to.

3. **If it was** cold, we remained indoors.

4. **If you earn** a little money, you spend it at once.

5. **If she were to learn** the truth, she would forgive him at once.

D. Traduire la proposition conditionnelle par une forme verbale à l'impératif.

Modèle: If you follow this route, you will end up near the cliffs.
- ● ***Suivez*** *cette route, vous vous retrouverez près des falaises.*
  impératif

---

1. **If you are** absolutely sincere, you will be respected.

2. **If she adheres to** this diet, she will lose a lot of weight.

3. **If you ask** questions, you stand to learn far more.

4. **If he finishes** this painting, the gallery may purchase it.

5. **If we consult** our lawyer, our chances for winning the case increase considerably.

E. Traduire la proposition conditionnelle par *sans, n'était* (ou *n'eût été*) + substantif ou pronom.

Modèle: **Were it not for** his friend's ardent devotion, that man would be an altogether different person.

● ***Sans** l'ardent dévouement de son ami, cet homme serait une personne tout autre.*
  sans   +   substantif

---

  1. **Had it not been for** the war, innumerable ancient monuments could still be seen today.

  2. **If it were not for** her work, she would have more time for her family.

  3. I could not have endured these past weeks, **if it had not been for** you.

  4. **If it had not been for** the family's devoted care, she would probably not have recovered.

  5. **Were it not for** inflation, his pension would provide him with a comfortable income.

F. Traduire en remplaçant la proposition conditionnelle par un adjectif ou un substantif en apposition.

Modèle: **If it were smaller and more economical,** this car would interest us.

● ***Plus petite et plus économique,** cette voiture nous intéresserait.*
  adjectifs (épithètes détachées)

---

  1. **As a wife and mother,** she appears perfectly happy.

  2. **Had I been a novelist,** I too could have become rich and famous.

  3. **Were you wealthy,** you would no longer need to work.

  4. **As a truck driver,** he would earn twice the salary he earns as a professor.

  5. **If she were a college graduate,** she could find a better-paying job.

G. Traduire en remplaçant la proposition conditionnelle par un participe présent.

Modèle: That young woman is remarkably beautiful; most men, **if they passed** her on the street, would be overcome with admiration.

● *Cette jeune femme est une vraie beauté; la plupart des hommes, la **croisant** dans la rue, seraient frappés d'admiration.*   participe présent

---

  1. Anyone, **if he heard** her story, would feel envious of her.

  2. Many people, **if they met** that author, would be impressed by her brilliance.

  3. Most critics, **if they read** his play, would miss the point entirely.

  4. **If children saw** such a film, they would have nightmares.

  5. **Were his friends to discover** the truth, they would react rather violently to certain assumptions.

H. Traduire la phrase conditionnelle par deux propositions à l'infinitif, liées par *c'est.*

Modèle: **If you walk** in this park early in the morning, **you feel** a profound sense of peace.

● *Se promener tôt le matin dans ce parc, c'est connaître un calme profond.*
  infinitif   *c'est* + infinitif

1. **If you flout** the conventions of society, **you court** disaster.

2. **If you betray** a friend, **you betray** yourself.

3. **If you left** him alone, **you would be doing** him a great favor.

4. **If you judged** her without hearing her side, **you would be committing** a grave injustice.

5. **Taking** responsibility for your own acts **is living** as a free person.

I. Traduire la proposition conditionnelle par une locution prépositive + substantif (ou infinitif).

Modèle: If there is a fire, go to the window and make your presence known.

● *En cas d'incendie, manifestez votre présence à la fenêtre.*
  locution prépositive
      + substantif

Modèle: If the child puts his room in order, he will be forgiven.

● *À condition de tout bien ranger dans sa chambre, l'enfant sera pardonné.*
  locution prépositive   +   infinitif

1. She can read Italian **if she looks up every other word in the dictionary.**

2. **If they did not have dowries,** many girls remained unmarried.

3. **If he had a large enough sum of money,** he would be able to discharge all his debts.

4. **If they were in need,** they would ask us to help them.

5. She makes a good impression, **if she says nothing.**

54 | PROPOSITION CONCESSIVE

A. Traduire la phrase concessive par deux propositions comportant des verbes au conditionnel présent ou passé, liées ou non par *que* facultatif.

Modèle: Even if the house had collapsed, the workman would have been completely unaware of it.

● *La maison se serait effondrée que l'ouvrier en aurait été tout à fait inconscient.*
  verbe au conditionnel   verbe au conditionnel

1. **If the painting had been** unsigned, **we would have guessed** the name of the painter nonetheless.

2. **Even if she were** penniless, **she would** never **ask** him for anything.

3. **If she were** a great success, **it would still** not **change** her.

4. **Even if he told** me himself, **I would** not **believe it.**

5. **Even if you worked** all night, **you would** not **be able** to finish it in time.

B. Traduire la proposition concessive par *quitte à* ou *sauf à* + infinitif.

Modèle: The citizens intoned their revolutionary songs **even though they risked being shot down** by soldiers of the republic.

- *Les citoyens psalmodiaient leurs chants révolutionnaires, **quitte à être fusillés** par les soldats de la république.*　　　　　　　　　　　　　　　　　　*quitte à* + infinitif

---

1. Many couples marry in haste, **even though they might be sorry** later.

2. She remained true to her principles, **even though she might be persecuted** by society.

3. **Even at the risk of hurting** others, he always tells the truth.

4. **Though she risks becoming** seriously ill, she insists on performing tonight.

5. His secretary rejected his advances, **even though she risked losing** her job.

C. Traduire la proposition concessive par *quitte à* ou *sauf à* + infinitif. Comparer avec les phrases de l'exercice précédant et noter la différence de sens.

Modèle: I am giving up teaching, **but I may take it up again** a few years from now.

- *Je renonce à l'enseignement, **quitte à le reprendre** d'ici quelques années.*
quitte à + infinitif

---

1. Could we interrupt this discussion **and continue it** this afternoon?

2. She always makes sacrifices **and then boasts about it** afterward.

3. He is retiring, **but he may start a new career** later on.

4. The workers are calling off the strike, **with the understanding that they are to obtain a substantial increase** in salary.

5. Management makes magnificent promises, **only to renege on them** subsequently.

D. Traduire la proposition concessive par *pour* + infinitif.

Modèle: **Although** that student **spent** two years in France, he does not possess a thorough knowledge of the country.

- *Pour avoir passé deux ans en France, cet étudiant ne possède pas une connaissance appro-*
  pour + infinitif
  fondie du pays.

---

1. **Although she has tried** every conceivable diet, she is still overweight.

2. This car, **though it is** old and dilapidated, is nonetheless an excellent bargain.

3. **Though they have suffered** many hardships, the refugees remain cheerful and hopeful.

4. This roast is still tasty, **though it is** overcooked.

5. These students are not certain of passing the examinations, **although they have worked** assiduously.

E. Traduire la proposition concessive par *sans* + infinitif, présent ou passé.

Modèle: This orator, **though he may not move** the masses, possesses a radiant charisma.

- *Cet orateur, **sans émouvoir** les masses, est doué d'un charisme lumineux.*
  sans + infinitif

---

1. **Although he has not finished** high school, this writer has read all the great books of world literature.

2. **Although she has no** children of her own, that doctor considers herself an authority on child rearing.

3. She is willing to marry him for his money, **although she does not love** him.

4. Professor Duval, the famous linguist, speaks seventeen foreign languages, **although he has never visited** the countries where they are spoken.

5. That man, **although he is not** handsome, is the most enchanting person I have ever met.

F. Traduire la proposition concessive par une simple apposition (substantif en apposition ou épithète détachée).

Modèle: **Although she is a queen,** people like her because of her unaffectedness.

- *Reine, elle plaît par sa simplicité.*
  apposition

---

1. **Whether it is true or false,** that remark is hilariously funny.

2. **Although he was a mere peasant,** he received the greatest honors his country could bestow.

3. **Whether he is a genius or a charlatan,** he is thought to be responsible for a number of miraculous cures.

4. **Although he was hideous and deformed,** Quasimodo was capable of the purest, most tender love.

5. **Although she is only of average intelligence,** she daydreams about becoming a great scientist.

G. Traduire la proposition concessive par *avoir beau* + infinitif.

Modèle: Although the prompter tries to help the poor actress, she misses every cue.

- *Le souffleur a beau essayer d'aider la pauvre actrice, elle rate toutes ses répliques.*
  avoir beau + infinitif

---

1. **Although his mother keeps urging** him to practice, that child remains uninterested in music.

2. **Although she tries** to remain inconspicuous, her beauty draws attention to her everywhere.

3. The actor refused to take another curtain call, **although the audience continued to applaud.**

4. **However much you try** to provoke the dog, he will ignore you.

5. **Although her designs are** original and brilliant, they fail to sell well.

H. Traduire la proposition concessive par *tout en* + participe présent.

Modèle: Although the newly married man **worked only** twenty hours a week, he managed to get rich.

- *Le jeune marié, **tout en ne travaillant que** vingt heures par semaine, arrivait à s'enrichir.*
  tout en + participe
  présent

---

1. **Although he fills** his days with activities of all kinds, he still finds time for his family and friends.

2. She is completely unaware of her underlying motivations, **although she analyzes herself** constantly.

3. **Even though he jogs** every day, he still has not lost enough weight.

4. **Although we eat** three satisfying meals a day, we still can lose weight.

5. **Even though she refuses** to practice stringent economy, she somehow manages to make ends meet.

I. Traduire la proposition concessive par une préposition + substantif.

Modèle: Although her devoutness was deep-seated, she could not help but have doubts about the existence of God.

- *Malgré sa dévotion foncière, elle ne pouvait s'empêcher de douter de l'existence de Dieu.*
  préposition + substantif

---

1. **Although she is in excellent health,** she prefers to lead a sedentary life.

2. **Although his wife was a gourmet cook,** he never put on weight.

3. **Though he was fluent in the language,** the student found it difficult to adjust to life in a foreign country.

4. **Though she is well known and loved,** she remains basically shy and modest.

5. **Even though she has a cold,** she looks as lovely as ever.

J. Traduire la proposition concessive par une proposition principale, en laissant tomber la conjonction concessive et en introduisant l'autre proposition par *cependant, pourtant, néanmoins,* ou *toutefois,* précédé ou non de *mais* ou *et.*

Modèle: **Although** the former actor fancied himself to be the future president, he **nevertheless** did not even dare run for office.

- *L'ancien comédien se croyait le futur président, (**mais**) **pourtant** il n'a même pas osé se porter candidat à l'élection.*

---

1. **Although** he made an early start, he **nonetheless** arrived late.

2. **Although** she has a slight stammer, she is determined to become a great public speaker.

3. **Though** they have lost all their earthly possessions, they have **nevertheless** attained serenity and optimism.

4. **Although** we have been waiting for an hour, no one has served us yet.

5. **Although** he is the greatest living expert in his field, in other respects he is as naive as a child.

55 | PROPOSITION CAUSALE

A. Traduire la proposition causale par *pour* + infinitif passé.

Modèle: The prince is not well regarded by his people **because he married** the daughter of a rich bourgeois.

- *Le prince est mal vu de son peuple **pour avoir épousé** la fille d'un riche bourgeois.*

$$pour + \begin{array}{l} \text{infinitif} \\ \text{passé} \end{array}$$

---

1. **Because she overslept,** she missed the nine o'clock train.

2. They are world-famous **because they crossed** the Atlantic Ocean on a raft.

3. Dr. Salk is known and respected **because he discovered** a cure for polio.

4. I know this film by heart **because I have seen it** ten times.

5. People loved the president **because he helped** the poor and the underprivileged.

B. Traduire la proposition causale par *de* + infinitif.

Modèle: I was stupefied **because I perceived** the two scars on his hands.
- *De lui **découvrir** les deux cicatrices aux mains, j'en restais stupéfaite.*
  de + infinitif

1. She felt apprehensive **at the mere thought** of finding two white hairs above her left temple.

2. He rejoiced **because he had recovered** his wallet.

3. The young actress is smiling **because she anticipates** tomorrow's triumph.

4. **Upon recalling** the critics' laudatory comments, he trembled with delight.

5. We are very happy **because we have** at last **received** news from them.

C. Traduire la proposition causale par un participe présent.

Modèle: The dentist refuses to see his patients socially **because he considers** them vulgar.
- *Le dentiste refuse la fréquentation de ses clients, les **considérant** grossiers.*
  participe
  present

1. That driver, **because he was** in a hurry, went through a red light and received a traffic summons.

2. **Since she knows** how to swim, she is not afraid of the water.

3. He committed an imprudent act **because he lost** his head.

4. **Because she feels** inferior to her classmates, she assumes a boisterous, aggressive manner.

5. **Because they wished** to avoid war, they pursued a dangerous policy of appeasement.

D. Traduire la proposition causale par un adjectif (épithète détachée) ou un substantif en apposition.

Modèle: Because they were great jazz fans, the instrumentalists organized a trip to New Orleans.
- ***Grands amateurs de jazz,** les instrumentistes organisèrent un voyage à la Nouvelle-Orléans.*
  substantif en apposition

1. **Because he is a perfectionist,** he winces at the slightest error.

2. The Sorbonne, **because it is known worldwide,** attracts students from all nations.

3. She trusted her children and respected their wishes **because she was a devoted mother.**

4. **Because he proved to be an effective leader,** he was reelected by a landslide.

5. **Because they are too lenient,** many high school teachers are unable to maintain discipline in their classrooms.

E. Traduire la proposition causale par une locution prépositive + infinitif.

Modèle: **Because it fears the displeasure** of its customers, the firm allows them to buy on credit.

• *Par crainte de déplaire à ses clients, la maison leur permet d'acheter à terme.*
   locution prépositive   +   infinitif

---

1. The prime minister suffered a crushing defeat **because he failed to win** the confidence of the voters.

2. **Because we live** in an affluent society, we enjoy an exceptionally high standard of living.

3. **Because it claimed to be defending** the national interest, the administration spent enormous sums on armaments.

4. She refrained from contradicting him **because she did not wish to offend** him.

5. **Because he had worked** too hard and **slept** too little, he nearly forgot how to enjoy life.

56 | PROPOSITION CONSÉCUTIVE

A. Traduire la proposition consécutive par *à* + infinitif.

Modèle: The runners are so exhausted **that they can no longer stand up.**

• *Les coureurs sont recrus de fatigue à n'en plus pouvoir tenir debout.*
   à   +   infinitif

---

1. The clowns did such funny tricks **that you could have died laughing.***

2. She sang an old ballad so sad **that it could wring your heart.**

3. Her speech was greeted by applause so loud **it could deafen you.**

4. In this film there is one scene **funny enough to make you double over with laughter.***

5. We love seeing films so scary **that they could make your hair stand on end.**

B. Traduire la proposition consécutive en employant *être de* + substantif sans article + *à* + infinitif.

Modèle: The girl **is strong enough to defend herself** if need be.

• *La fille est de taille à se défendre si besoin est.*
   être de + substantif + *à* + infinitif

---

1. I **am not in the mood to jest.**

2. She **is not the sort of person who would hide** her true feelings.

3. The boy **is not big enough to fight** such an opponent.

4. Do you believe that a woman **would be strong enough to lift** such heavy weights?

5. I **am not the type to swallow** an insult without retaliating.

C. Traduire la proposition consécutive par *jusqu'à* + substantif ou infinitif, ou *au point de* + infinitif, ou *assez* + adjectif + *pour* + infinitif.

Modèle: The style in that author's work is **so** elaborate **that it becomes absurd.**
- *Chez cet auteur, le style est travaillé **jusqu'à l'absurdité.***

Modèle: The weather had been **so** good **that** all the vines **ripened** right at harvest time.
- *Le temps avait été propice **au point de faire mûrir** toutes les vignes juste à l'époque des vendanges.*

Modèle: The measures taken were timely **enough to allow** the university's normal opening.
- *Les mesures prises ont été **assez** opportunes **pour permettre** l'ouverture normale de l'université.*

---

1. She is **so** naive **that she believes** everything you tell her.

2. He was **so** charming **that he won** everyone's heart.

3. Her handwriting is **so** poor **that it is illegible.**

4. She was **so** courageous **that she could face** death without fear.

5. They were **so** much in love **that they forgot** all other considerations.

D. Traduire en faisant de la proposition consécutive la proposition principale, placée au début de la phrase, et en introduisant la deuxième proposition par *tant.*

Modèle: The employees have **so** much free time during the week **that they can take advantage of winter sports.**
- ***Les employés peuvent profiter des sports d'hiver tant** ils ont d'heures libres au cours de la semaine.*

---

1. He is **so** delighted by the results of the elections **that he has brought home two bottles of champagne.**

2. I am **so** sleepy **that I can no longer keep my eyes open.**

3. She drank and ate **so** much **that she fell asleep at the table.**

4. The weather is **so** beautiful **that no one feels like working.**

5. That child is **so** intelligent **that she is always first in her class.**

57 | CONJONCTIONS: REMARQUES DIVERSES

A. Traduire *although* par *quelque . . . que, pour . . . que, si . . . que* ou *tout . . . que;* mettre le verbe au mode convenable.

Modèle: **Although certain specific poems are admirable,** the collection itself is somewhat slim.
- *Quelqu'admirables (Si admirables) que soient certains poèmes particuliers, le recueil même manque d'ampleur.*

Modèle: **Although she is honest (Honest though she may be),** she sometimes lies to please her friends.
- *Tout honnête qu'elle est (qu'elle soit), elle ment parfois pour faire plaisir à ses amis.*

1. **Although his explanation seems fishy,** it is the gospel truth.

2. **As talented as she might be,** she has not yet had the success she deserves.

3. **Although he is very much in love,** he is not blind to the faults of his beloved.

4. **As rich as they might now be,** they will never forget the poverty of their childhood years.

5. **Male chauvinist though he may be,** he cannot prevent his wife's active participation in the women's liberation movement.

B. Traduire *if but, if only, if . . . at all, if . . . slightly,* etc. par *pour peu que* + verbe au subjonctif.

Modèle: **If the pioneers of the Wild West had hesitated even slightly,** they would have been lost.
- *Pour peu que les pionniers du Far West eussent hésité, ils étaient perdus.*

1. **If he had respected her at all,** he would not have asked her to act against her conscience.

2. **If you criticize her children the slightest bit,** she becomes a tigress.

3. **Just by trying a little,** they might have succeeded.

4. **If a girl but speaks to him,** he blushes.

5. **If her teacher gave her just a little encouragement,** she might work harder.

C. Traduire *although* par *sans que* + verbe au subjonctif.

Modèle: **Although** the daughter does not realize it, she is performing an act of charity by writing to her mother now and then.
- *Sans que la fille s'en rende compte, elle fait acte de charité en écrivant à sa mère de temps à autre.*

1. **Although** Marie-Anne's lover does not suspect it, he was seen leaving her house after midnight.

2. Many people worry about the housing crisis, **although** it may not affect them personally.

3. **Although** he has never spoken to me, I feel as if I have always known him.

4. The patient is making steady progress, **although** he does not take care of himself as he should.

5. **Although** she does not quite understand his feelings, she is willing to humor him.

D. Traduire *although* par deux propositions liées par *que.*

Modèle: Although the tenants might have wanted to move in, their apartment was still not available.

- *Les locataires auraient désiré emménager **que** leur appartement ne se trouvait pas encore disponible.*

---

1. **Although** she would have liked to attend the afternoon performance, all the seats were already sold out.

2. **Although** they hoped to take a cruise this winter, their budget did not permit it.

3. **Although** she might wish to shirk her responsibilities, she could not do it.

4. **Although** he might have preferred to hide the truth from his wife, he was unable to deceive her.

5. **Although** many citizens would like to avoid paying income tax, they would not dare to risk the consequences.

E. Traduire *until* par une expression autre que *jusqu'à ce que.*

Modèle: Until an accused person has been proved guilty, he is innocent.

- ***Tant qu'****on n'a pas établi la culpabilité d'un accusé, il est innocent.*

---

1. They kept their old car **until** it finally fell apart.*

2. **Until** he received the confirmation of his promotion, he lived in an agony of suspense.

3. In Paris, she spoke only French, drank French wines, and made many French friends, **until** finally she came to think of herself as French.

4. She watched the plane recede in the distance, **until** it seemed only an infinitesimal gold dot on the horizon.

5. The old watchmaker continued to practice his craft **until** his failing eyesight forced him to retire.

F. Traduire *not . . . until* par *ne . . . pas . . . avant de* + infinitif, *ne . . . pas . . . avant que* + verbe au subjonctif, ou *ne . . . que lorsque* + verbe à l'indicatif.

Modèle: Teachers do **not** leave their offices **until** they finish correcting papers.

- *Le professeur **ne** quitte **pas** son bureau **avant d'**avoir terminé ses corrections.*

---

1. Many believe that criminals ought **not** to be released from prison **until** they have served their full sentences.

2. The age of reason will **not** begin **until** mankind has abolished war.

3. Marcel was **not** able to fall asleep **until** his mother had given him his ritual goodnight kiss.

4. The candidate swears that he will **not** rest **until** he has wiped out corruption in government.

5. She will **not** understand a mother's feelings **until** she is a mother herself.

G. Traduire *and, also, furthermore* par *d'autre part, du reste, d'ailleurs, de plus, en plus;* éviter *aussi* en début de proposition.

Modèle: The lawn has to be mowed. **Also,** the field needs weeding.

- *Le gazon est à tondre. **En plus,** le champ a besoin d'être sarclé.*

1. She is extraordinarily talented. She is **also** beautiful.

2. The faucet is leaking; **furthermore,** the washing machine needs repairing.

3. He is majoring in Oriental languages—**and** he is interested in Eastern religions.

4. The poor of this city are ill-fed and ill-housed. **Also,** many of them are unemployed.

5. We were delayed by bad weather and heavy traffic; we **also** had a flat tire.

H. Traduire *nor* (ou *neither*) en début de phrase par *d'ailleurs* ou *du reste* + verbe à la forme négative, ou par *ne . . . pas davantage* ou *ne. . . pas non plus.*

Modèle: **Nor** did the book have anything to do with the Hautier affair.

- *Le livre **n'**avait **du reste** rien à voir avec l'affaire Hautier.*

1. They had never seen a mountain before. **Nor** had they seen a desert.

2. The patient was forbidden to leave his bed for a week. **Nor** was he to eat red meat during that time.

3. She did not know how to cook. **Nor** could she sew.

4. He was unaware of his wife's charm. **Nor** did he appreciate her remarkable intelligence.

5. There are relatively few blacks in American medical schools. **Nor** are there many Orientals.

Exercices de sélection

Pour tous ces exercices, discuter et comparer vos choix.

A. (50, 51) Traduire les mots en caractères gras par au moins deux constructions différentes.

Modèle: We believe **that he is competent.**

- *Nous **le** croyons **compétent.***
- *À notre avis, **il est compétent.***

- *Il nous semble **compétent**.*
- *Nous croyons **à sa compétence**.*

---

1. I hope **that you will have a pleasant vacation.**

2. He insists **that his students work seriously and understand perfectly.**

3. We did not know **that they had so much courage.**

4. This woman claims **that she is a clairvoyant.**

5. They say **that he is a scrupulously honest man.**

6. He has to **revise the last three chapters of his book.**

7. She is afraid **that people will think she is a snob.**

8. Statisticians have proved **that there is a correlation between cigarette smoking and lung cancer.**

9. She used to imagine **that the South Seas islands were primitive and breathtakingly beautiful.**

10. His admirers believe **that he is a moviemaker of genius.**

B. (50, 52) Traduire les propositions temporelles par au moins deux constructions différentes.

Modèle: After peace had been declared, the nations showed their joy and happiness.
- *Après la déclaration de paix, les peuples manifestèrent leur joie et leur bonheur.*
- *Après avoir déclaré la paix, les peuples manifestèrent leur joie et leur bonheur.*
- *La paix déclarée, les peuples manifestèrent leur joie et leur bonheur.*
- *Une fois la paix déclarée, les peuples manifestèrent leur joie et leur bonheur.*

---

1. **Once she has been betrayed,** she will never again trust a person.

2. **After dessert was finished,** the chairman rose to present the speaker.

3. **Before she left,** she wrote a short note.

4. **As soon as his first volume of poetry was published,** it made him famous.

5. **When Mozart was a child,** he composed several pieces for the piano.

6. **As soon as the elections were over,** the president turned his attention to the international crisis.

7. **As she was on the verge of signing a new contract,** the ballerina discovered that she was pregnant.

8. **After he was condemned to die,** Villon wrote the famous ≪ Ballade des pendus ≫.

9. **When we reminisce about the good old days,** we forfeit the precious here-and-now.

10. **Once the slaves had been freed and the war ended,** the divided nation devoted itself to the task of reconstruction.

C. (50, 53) Traduire les propositions conditionnelles par au moins deux constructions différentes.

Modèle: If he were to run for president, he would be defeated.
- *Se proposerait-il comme candidat à la présidence,* *il ne serait pas élu.*
- *S'il se proposait comme candidat à la présidence,* *il ne serait pas élu.*
- *Qu'il se propose comme candidat à la présidence,* *il ne serait pas élu.*

---

1. **If you knew him,** you would respect him.

2. **If she were an actress,** she would be a great star.

3. **If it had not been for his associate's help,** he could not have conceived the plan.

4. **If he enters the contest,** he will surely win.

5. **If one is not dressed appropriately,** one may not enter the cathedral.

6. **If an emergency should arise,** I can be reached at the following address.

7. **If you smoke,** you are refused admittance to my apartment.

8. **If someone met her for the first time,** he would think that she was lively and cheerful.

9. They may sublet my apartment this summer, **on condition that they feed my cat and water my geraniums.**

10. **If he were single,** he would quit his job and return to school.

D. (50, 54, 57) Traduire les propositions concessives par au moins deux constructions différentes.

Modèle: Although she works hard, she is not always successful.
- *Elle a beau travailler dur,* *elle ne réussit pas toujours.*
- *Elle travaille dur, et cependant* *elle ne réussit pas toujours.*
- *Tout en travaillant dur,* *elle ne réussit pas toujours.*
- *Malgré son travail assidu,* *elle ne réussit pas toujours.*
- *Tout travailleuse qu'elle est,* *elle ne réussit pas toujours.*

---

1. **Although he has never traveled,** he speaks nine languages.

2. **Although they try to save money,** they cannot stay within their income.

3. **Although she is terrified of insects,** she refuses to kill them.

4. This aspiring actor, **although he is not handsome,** possesses extraordinary sex appeal.

5. **Although she is shy and unattractive,** she dreams of romance.

6. **Whether she is happy or sad,** she always wears a smile.

7. **Although he believes in God,** he never goes to church.

8. **Although we have been friends for a long time,** he has never asked me for a favor.

9. **Even though she cleans house three hours a day,** she is perpetually dissatisfied with the results.

10. **Though he is talented,** that painter lacks vision and imagination.

E. (50, 55) Traduire la proposition causale par au moins deux constructions différentes.

Modèle: Our young colleague deserves recognition **because he has worked tirelessly on our behalf.**

- *Notre jeune collègue mérite notre reconnaissance **pour avoir travaillé inlassablement dans notre intérêt.***

- *Notre jeune collègue mérite notre reconnaissance **car il a travaillé inlassablement dans notre intérêt.***

- *Notre jeune collègue, **ayant travaillé inlassablement dans notre intérêt,** mérite notre reconnaissance.*

1. **Because he is an outstanding athlete,** he is in training for the Olympics.

2. **Because she is a compulsive housewife,** she dusts and polishes even the doorknobs.

3. She was a celebrity **because she swam across the English Channel.**

4. The game is over **because there are no players left.**

5. He will drive very carefully **because he is afraid of causing an accident.**

6. **Because she is a caring person,** she is trusted by all.

7. She was dumbfounded, **because she suddenly glimpsed, in his hand, a flashing diamond wristwatch.**

8. **Because he knew the uncertainty of human destiny,** he refused to take anything seriously.

9. The mayor is unpopular **because he has broken all his campaign promises.**

10. **Because she is a loyal friend,** she stubbornly rejects the evidence compiled against him.

F. (50, 56) Traduire la proposition consécutive par au moins deux constructions différentes.

Modèle: He is **so** tired **that he can no longer walk.**

- *Il est recru de fatigue **à ne plus pouvoir marcher.***
- ***Il ne peut plus marcher tant** il est fatigué.*
- *Il est **trop** fatigué **pour marcher davantage.***
- *Il est fatigué **au point de ne plus pouvoir marcher.***
- *Recru de fatigue, **il ne peut plus marcher.***

1. The film was **so** scary **that it made us tremble.**

2. The weather is **so** hot **that no one feels like working.**

3. He was **so** furious **that he could not articulate a single word.**

4. The child is not strong **enough to defend himself.**

5. That girl's language is **so** gracious **that it becomes mannered to the point of preciosity.**

6. The price of gasoline was rising **so** steadily **that many motorists stopped driving on weekends.**

7. The ice, heavy **enough to bring down trees and power lines,** caused severe damage throughout the area.

8. The strike lasted long **enough to inconvenience thousands of vacationing tourists.**

9. The leading lady acted **so** convincingly **that she held her audience spellbound.**

10. The clown performed antics **so** funny **that you could split your sides laughing.***

G. (57) Traduire la proposition en caractères gras par au moins deux constructions différentes.

Modèle: He will **not** leave **until he has seen the editor.**
- *Il ne partira **que lorsqu'il aura vu le rédacteur en chef.***
- *Il ne partira **pas avant d'avoir vu le rédacteur en chef.***
- *Il ne partira **pas sans avoir vu le rédacteur en chef.***
- *Il ne partira **pas jusqu'à ce qu'il ait vu le rédacteur en chef.***

---

1. **Although this poet is a genius,** he is almost completely unknown.

2. His friends will **not** rest **until the critics have fully recognized his worth.**

3. She becomes enraged **if anyone disagrees with her even slightly.**

4. **Although the father and son do not realize it,** this is to be their last meeting.

5. The applicant has had no experience. **Nor does he seem particularly bright.**

6. The violinist has a very poor sense of rhythm. **Also, he plays off-key.**

7. **Although the workers are discontented,** they do not dare to strike.

8. **Until the union can obtain a more favorable contract,** it will continue the negotiations.

9. **If the tightrope walker had hesitated even the slightest bit,** she could have lost her balance.

10. **Although they would have liked to take the seven o'clock flight,** the plane was full.

Exercices de synthèse

A. Sur une feuille séparée, traduire les phrases suivantes en utilisant les techniques suggérées dans le chapitre consacré à la conjonction. (Vu la complexité du sujet, il y a deux séries de trente phrases.)

Série 1

1. When that lesson was done, we knew much more about the subjunctive.
2. Although Monday has arrived, I'm still not ready for work.
3. As soon as they got here, they ran to the window, and when they saw her coming, they let me know.
4. Once a human being has become accustomed to a vegetarian diet, he can live on it almost indefinitely.
5. If it had not been for you, I would have been lost.
6. Except for the way he pronounced his *r,* you would have thought him British.
7. I have only to find him nervous and angry, and I know what has happened.
8. At the time she was ill, all her friends rallied around her.
9. When I touched the fur of that coat, I quivered with pleasure.
10. While I am alive, you shall lack nothing; but after I am dead, beware.
11. When I hear him talking like that, I recall the first time that I visited his home.
12. If we learn without much effort, we know without appreciating our knowledge.
13. You may have this book, on the condition that you take good care of it.
14. There is no doubt that gregariousness is a very common human trait.
15. I thought that I had told them how important my work was.
16. I was certainly astonished that you should want to share in his glory.
17. She had a habit of interrupting and answering even before she knew what I was going to say.
18. She always wants people to take her for an aristocrat.
19. What chance do you think I have of winning?
20. If we can take your word for it, all of them are honest.
21. Why should you doubt what I say? Do you think you are smarter than I?
22. Serious difficulties were created for us when they left so suddenly.
23. We are very far from wishing to contradict you.
24. Now they are sorry that they behaved badly while they were in Rome.
25. After the strike was over, the union believed that it had succeeded in obtaining a fair settlement.
26. Although she reads many books, she is amazingly ignorant of current events.
27. They must present their tickets, passports, and visas before they board the ship.
28. She thought he had such great courage that he could tell the whole truth unflinchingly.
29. I cannot believe that she is capable of such heroism.
30. When he was a mature man, Leblanc repudiated all that he had written as an adolescent.

Série 2

1. Although bound by my promise, I had no intention of offending anyone.
2. Although you change the words, take care not to change the meaning.
3. She walked slowly out the door, as if she were overwhelmed by the weight of responsibility.
4. In spite of his being unusually young, you could recognize that he had a certain indefinable maturity.
5. Even if I had never seen him, I would have recognized him by his mischievous smile.
6. I did not want her to miss the last train home.
7. I doubt that anyone is in the room, since the papers on my desk are undisturbed.
8. She emptied her glass upon the ground, only to refill it when my back was turned.
9. Although we looked everywhere, we found no trace of her activities.
10. The general lost the battle because he did not have the time necessary to bring up reinforcements.
11. Even if he were a thousand times more charming, I would not fall in love with him.

12. At school, since I was a very ordinary pupil, no one paid any special attention to me.
13. As he was very much in love, he noticed none of the faults of his lover.
14. You are not old enough to understand what we are talking about.
15. My plans, although they are quite unambitious, are still rather important to me. [*deux façons*]
16. I should have told her to her face what I thought of her, even though I would have had to pay dearly for it.
17. The bear's teeth were sharp enough to bite right through an iron rod.
18. Although a dictator may be very powerful, he cannot long force a people against its will.
19. If he cared for her at all, he would want her to be strong and independent, even at the risk of losing her.
20. I shall stay here watching you until you do as I ask.
21. The owner did not tell us that the roof was leaking; nor did we know about the crack in the beam.
22. I am so happy that I feel like singing and dancing.
23. She says she cannot finish the exercise until she gets a better dictionary.
24. She did not tell me anything about it until it was all done.
25. They say he is so poor that he does not know where his next meal is coming from.
26. If she had believed that he was guilty, she could not have defended him so convincingly. Nor would she have continued to live with him under the same roof.
27. Since they love skiing, they are planning a trip to Vermont, even though the trails are in poor condition this winter.
28. We believe that the economic crisis is so severe that each and every one of us will soon feel its impact.
29. The wrecking crew will not blow up the building until everyone has been evacuated.
30. His mother did not feel that he was mature enough to live alone. Also, she wished to keep him tied to her apron strings.

B. Sur une feuille séparée, traduire ce passage en tenant compte autant que possible des techniques étudiées jusqu'à présent.

I was so weary when I arrived back at my apartment, and my spirits were so low, that I wanted to telephone Suzanne and break our date for dinner. . . . But I found I simply didn't have enough energy to dial her number and go through the endless arguments that would inevitably ensue. So I had a cup of warmed-over coffee, which tasted vile yet somehow helped me to continue living; then I soaked in a hot bath for twenty minutes, and lo and behold, I came out of it feeling almost human again. . . .

I was just putting on a new party dress of sheer black wool by Trigère, which I'd acquired for a song from the assistant buyer in the Boutique on the third floor (because some heavy-handed customer had pulled a seam open) when the doorbell rang. It was Suzanne, looking marvelous in a light blue Givenchy cape, which I hadn't seen before, laughing at me and saying "Surprise,* d'Arcy! Surprise!"

Surprise, surprise, indeed. She'd brought two men with her (if I hadn't been exhausted I might have guessed she was planning* something like this), and I still required ten minutes of concentrated work before I was fit to be seen by anyone of the opposite sex. I ushered them into the living room, told Suzanne to fix them a drink, and dashed into* my bedroom to complete the task of making myself, if not irresistible, at least presentable. In a little while she joined me, carrying a Martini for herself and one for me. She sat down on my bed smirking.

"You could have warned me you were bringing men," I said, trying to sound wounded and indignant.

"And spoiled the surprise?" Suzanne said. "Pooh. Besides, you looked charming, with your hair wild and your dress open at the back. The two gentlemen were very impressed."

Bernard Glemser, *Here Come the Brides*
(New York: Bantam, 1971), pp. 47–50.

9 | L'ORDRE DES MOTS

Assimilation des structures

58 | POSITION DE L'OBJET

A. Traduire en employant un pronom objet devant le verbe de façon à pouvoir placer le substantif objet au début de la phrase.

---

             objet   verbe

Modèle: Certain facts we refuse to admit.

- *Certains faits, nous refusons de **les** admettre.*
    substantif   pronom + verbe
    objet   objet

---

1. **That woman** I can't stand.*

2. **The murderer's name** we already know.

3. **These truths** we hold sacred.

4. He did not touch the food, but **the wine** he drank.

5. **The letter and the photographs** you may keep, if you wish.

B. Mettre la phrase au passif, de façon à placer le substantif objet devant le verbe, et ainsi faire de l'objet un sujet.

---

            verbe actif + substantif objet

Modèle: Le public ne tolère plus *cette façon de jouer.*

- ***Cette façon de jouer** n'est plus tolérée par le public.*
    sujet passif   verbe passif

---

1. Un grand nombre de touristes visitent tous les jours *la Tour Eiffel.*

2. Les étudiants ne respectent guère *un professeur trop indulgent.*

3. Plusieurs anthropologues ont étudié *les aborigènes d'Australie.*

4. L'auteur a omis *de nombreux faits importants.*

5. Un jour, le monde entier reconnaîtra *la grandeur de ce pays.*

C. Traduire en utilisant *c'est . . . que.*

---

objet   sujet + verbe
Modèle: It was a veritable fortune that my best friend won.

    • *Ce fut une véritable fortune que gagna ma meilleure amie.*

            objet   verbe   +   sujet

---

1. **It was his love and not his money that** his family wanted.

2. **It is good food and good wine that** the gourmet values.

3. **It is his plays and not his novels that** the public admires.

4. **It is her sense of humor that** her colleagues appreciate.

5. **It is power and not wisdom that** our contemporaries seek.

D. Traduire en utilisant une expression figée comportant un substantif objet qui précède le verbe.

---

                     verbe + objet

Modèle: He yielded **without striking a blow.**

    • *Il céda **sans coup férir.***

            objet + verbe

---

1. They consented **very reluctantly.**

2. He went away **without saying a word.**

3. In the winter, the ground freezes **hard.**

4. **On the way,** she encountered an old friend whom she had not seen for a long time.

5. Abandon my children? **God forbid!**

E. Traduire, puis justifier la position du pronom objet.

Modèle: He wishes to hear **her.**

    • *Il veut **l**'entendre.*

      objet

    Justification: le pronom objet précède l'infinitif.

Modèle: He hears **her** singing.

    • *Il **l**'entend chanter.*

      objet

    Justification: l'infinitif est précédé du verbe *entendre,* donc l'objet précède ce verbe.

---

1. She cannot do **it.**

2. I see **them** coming.

3. They will have **it** built. (house)

4. We would like to help **him.**

5. She let **him** leave without saying a word.

F. Traduire en utilisant *faire* + infinitif + substantif objet.

Modèle: City planners have **entire neighborhoods** rebuilt.

● *Les urbanistes font reconstruire **des quartiers entiers.***
      faire + infinitif + substantif objet

1. We had **the roof** repaired.

2. She has **her hair and her eyebrows** dyed.

3. He had **a tennis racket** replaced.

4. These wealthy matrons have all **their clothes** made by *haute couture* designers.

5. To have **his driver's license** renewed, he will have to have new **eyeglasses** made.

G. Traduire en employant *laisser, entendre, sentir, voir*, etc. + infinitif + substantif objet de l'infinitif.

Modèle: The travelers hear **a Verdian melody** being hummed.

● *Les voyageurs entendent fredonner **une mélodie verdienne.***
      entendre + infinitif + substantif objet

1. We heard *La Marseillaise* being sung.

2. The witnesses saw **the document** being signed.

3. She is watching **the flag** being raised.

4. He would never allow **an injustice** to be committed.

5. Raptly, the composer was listening to **his sonata** being played.

H. Traduire en employant *laisser, entendre, sentir, voir*, etc. + infinitif + substantif sujet de l'infinitif.

Modèle: The travelers hear **a baritone** humming.

● *Les voyageurs entendent fredonner **un baryton.***
      entendre + infinitif + substantif sujet

1. One can almost feel **time** passing.

2. The passers-by watched **the painter** working.

3. Listen to **the nightingale** singing!

4. Surprised, she let all **her bundles** drop.

5. On Sunday morning you can hear **the church bells** ringing.

I. Traduire en employant *laisser, entendre, sentir, voir,* etc. Placer le substantif sujet devant l'infinitif, puis justifier cette position.

Modèle: The tourists observe **the artisan working** with extreme care.

- *Les touristes observent **l'artisan travailler** avec un soin extrême.*
  substantif sujet + infinitif

Justification: cet ordre permet à l'infinitif de précéder directement un complément circonstanciel.

Modèle: You can hear **the child calling.**

- *On entend **l'enfant appeler.***
  substantif + infinitif
  sujet

Justification: cet ordre évite l'ambiguïté de *On entend appeler l'enfant.*

---

1. She heard **the children laughing** uproariously.

2. Let **that poor man finish** his work without interruption.

3. He saw **all the actors applauding.**

4. The musing poet watched **the young lovers walking** together hand in hand.

5. I felt **my heart beating** rapidly.

J. Traduire, puis justifier l'ordre des objets.

Modèle: The lawyer entrusted all the money **to the daughter.**

- *L'avocat remit tous les fonds **à la fille.***
  verbe + objet direct + objet indirect

Justification: l'objet direct précède l'objet indirect (règle générale).

Modèle: The lawyer entrusted **to the eldest** the money that should have been shared among several brothers and sisters.

- *L'avocat remit **à l'aîné** les fonds qui auraient dû être partagés entre plusieurs frères et sœurs.*
  objet + objet + proposition
  indirect   direct   relative

Justification: l'objet indirect précède l'objet direct, pour permettre à l'objet direct d'être suivi immédiatement par son complément (ici une proposition relative).

---

1. The real estate agent showed the house **to his clients.**

2. The real estate agent showed **his clients** a two-story brick house.

3. He prefers the humble abode built by his ancestors in a small Anjou village **to all the palaces of Rome.**

4. The great scholar possesses, **in addition to his vast learning,** a rare and endearing modesty. [*joindre à*]

5. The guide was relating the history of that painting **to his unenthusiastic audience.**

K. Traduire en plaçant le complément en caractères gras devant le verbe ou le substantif auquel il est lié. Justifier cette position exceptionnelle.

Modèle: The child already showed himself a remarkably discriminating judge **of painting.**

• *L'enfant montrait déjà **de la peinture** une appréciation remarquable et fine.*
   complément déterminatif + substantif

Justification: l'objet direct, plus long et plus important, occupe la position finale accentuée.

---

1. He prefers a painful, demanding struggle for perfection **to an easy mediocrity.**

2. I will always cherish the memory **of this evening.**

3. The farmers sell their freshest fruits and vegetables **to restaurant owners.**

4. She has an insatiable appetite **for flattery.**

5. She submits more easily **to great calamities** than to the petty irritations of everyday living.

---

59 | POSITION DE L'ADVERBE ET DU COMPLÉMENT CIRCONSTANCIEL

A. Traduire en faisant attention à la position relative des compléments circonstanciels.

Modèle: One spring evening, the village, still sleepy from winter, burst out in celebration.

• *Par un soir de printemps dans le village encore ensommeillé sous l'effet de l'hiver, la fête éclata.*

---

1. On the stroke of midnight, on the steps of the palace, a beautiful young girl, running frantically, dropped a glass slipper.

2. The two friends, engaged in animated conversation, strolled side by side in leisurely fashion along the embankments of the Seine.

3. One autumn evening on the Boulevard Saint-Michel, a satanic-looking man was sitting at a sidewalk café sipping a glass of Pernod.

4. The incident occurred at three o'clock in the afternoon, on the corner of a busy thoroughfare crowded with cars and people.

5. Once upon a time, many years ago in a faraway land, there lived a frail, green-eyed girl-child who possessed the gift of second sight.

B. Traduire en plaçant l'adverbe de quantité devant le participe passé ou l'infinitif.

Modèle: The team labored **very hard** and, fortunately, was **quite** successful.

- *L'équipe a **beaucoup** peiné et, heureusement, a **bien** réussi.*

1. She studied **so hard** the night before that she was exhausted on the day of the examination.

2. They have traveled **a lot** without learning **much.**

3. I have revealed **enough.**

4. He spoke **too much;** in fact, he had never spoken **so much** in his life.

5. We have suffered **very little.**

C. Traduire en plaçant l'adverbe indéfini de temps ou de lieu devant l'infinitif ou le participe passé.

Modèle: Certain people like to be begged **all the time.**

- *Certaines gens prennent plaisir **à toujours** se faire prier.*

1. They are going to leave **soon.**

2. **Often** I have wondered how that is done.

3. They waited **for a long time,** but **never** lost patience.

4. It is crucial to fight injustice **at all times and in all places.**

5. **Everywhere** we heard about his feats.

D. Traduire en plaçant l'adverbe de manière devant le participe passé.

Modèle: The journalist **at once** regretted the remark he had just addressed to his listeners.

- *Le journaliste a **instantanément** regretté la remarque qu'il venait d'adresser à ses auditeurs.*

1. He has changed his mind **completely.**

2. For the first time she **really** listened to what he was saying.

3. She **immediately** accepted his proposal.

4. The artist **carefully** added a few touches to his painting.

5. He has **evidently** forgotten our appointment.

E. Traduire en plaçant l'adverbe *bien, mal,* ou *mieux* devant l'infinitif ou le participe passé.

Modèle: The council made a proposal that was **well** received by its president.

- *Le conseil fit une proposition qui fut **bien** reçue par son président.*

1. He performed **quite well** and promised to do **even better** next time.

2. Gourmets attach great importance to eating and drinking **well.**

3. In order to understand her husband's work **better,** she is taking a chemistry course.

4. She looks for symbols in everything she reads, at the risk of interpreting the author's intentions **incorrectly.**

5. The novelist has developed his characters **well;** moreover, he has concretized the absurdity of the human condition **better** than any of his contemporaries.

F. Traduire en plaçant le complément circonstanciel de temps ou de manière entre le substantif sujet et le verbe.

Modèle: The journal's circulation **this year** is increasing by leaps and bounds.

- *Le tirage de la revue, **cette année**, va augmentant à une allure vertigineuse.*

substantif sujet	+	complément circonstanciel + verbe de temps

1. The salesgirl, **with a mechanical smile,** handed the wrapped package to the customer and wished her a pleasant day.

2. **At that time,** films were all silent and always in black and white.

3. **In the final year of his life,** the novelist completed his masterpiece.

4. **With a horrible screech of the brakes,** the taxi driver brought his vehicle to a sudden stop, barely avoiding a collision.

5. The villain, **with a leer,** twirled his moustache and advanced on tiptoe toward the sleeping heroine.

G. Traduire en intercalant l'adverbe ou le complément circonstanciel entre *ne* et *pas.* (Noter que l'adverbe suit le verbe ou, dans un temps composé, le verbe auxiliaire.)

Modèle: **Moreover,** the newspaper was not forced to replace its printers by machines.

- *Le journal n'a **du reste** pas été obligé de remplacer ses imprimeurs typographes par des machines automatiques.*

1. The union leaders will **certainly** not believe the company's vague promises.

2. **However,** they will not declare a strike without the support of the majority of the membership.

3. **Perhaps** he has not had time to consider your proposal carefully.

4. **Actually,** I do not approve of his political views.

5. The cost of living is **indeed** not declining but rising steadily.

H. Traduire en plaçant les pronoms indéfinis *rien* et *tout* devant l'infinitif ou le participe passé. (Noter, cependant, l'ordre exceptionnel dans *comme si de rien n'était.*)

---

verbe + pronom indéfini

Modèle: The witness refused to say **anything.**

- *Le témoin ne voulait **rien** dire.*

rien + infinitif

---

1. It is impossible to know **everything.**

2. She understood **everything** and she forgot **nothing.**

3. Ignoring the screams and the sirens, the professor calmly continued teaching the imperfect subjunctive **as if nothing were the matter.**

4. Since he has asked for **nothing,** he will get **nothing.**

5. They have told **everything** without omitting **anything.**

60 | INVERSION

A. Traduire en utilisant une formule optative (verbe au subjonctif suivi par le sujet).

Modèle: Long live France!   **May the tyrant perish!**
- *Vive la France!*   - *Périsse le tyran!*

---

1. **Long live the king!**

2. **Come springtime,** all will be well.

3. **May heaven grant** that they succeed!

4. **Long life to the newlyweds!**

5. **May you** live happily together for many, many years!

B. Traduire en utilisant *n'était* ou *n'eût été* + substantif sujet.

Modèle: If she were not so madly in love with him, she would have left him long ago.
- ***N'était l'amour insensé*** *qu'elle lui voue, elle l'aurait quitté il y a longtemps.*

---

1. **If he did not enjoy** his work so much, he would retire.

2. **Had it not been for her husband's loyal support,** she would not have had the courage to go on.

3. One would take him for a truck driver **if he were not so elegantly dressed.**

4. **Had it not been for the work** to which he devoted all his time, he could have spent more time with his family.

5. Those two women would be very lonely, **were it not for the devoted friendship** that they share.

C. Traduire en faisant l'inversion du sujet et du verbe après l'adverbe ou la conjonction.

Modèle: Thus began a new era for Europe, **at least so it was said.**
- *Ainsi débuta une ère nouvelle pour l'Europe, du moins l'affirma-t-on.*

1. **The war had hardly ended** when an epidemic of Spanish flu broke out all over Europe.

2. **Perhaps he is trying to show** how family life stifles the artist.

3. She has only one pair of gloves, **and even that one is torn!**

4. The price of gasoline is rising exorbitantly; **therefore, we must drive** as little as possible.

5. His mother treats him like a child of ten; **moreover, she reads** his mail!

D. Traduire en faisant l'inversion complexe: sujet + verbe + pronom sujet.

Modèle: Perhaps the wind will abate.
- *Peut-être le vent se calmera-t-il.*
        sujet + verbe + pronom sujet

1. It was dusk; **the sun had barely set.**

2. There is only one man who noticed the machine's flaw, **and even that person is unwilling to admit it.**

3. **Perhaps this candidate will try** to prove himself a true statesman.

4. **Perhaps the cost of living will go down; at least the newspapers predict** an economic recession in the near future.

5. Many famous writers have been regular patrons of this café; **therefore, tourists flock to it.**

E. Traduire en faisant l'inversion verbe + sujet dans la proposition relative.

Modèle: The pilgrims saw before them the saint **that numberless crusaders had venerated** in the past.
- *Les pèlerins virent devant eux le saint qu'avaient vénéré d'innombrables croisés d'autrefois.*

1. She does not realize the emotions **that her thoughtless words arouse.**

2. In this forest, one finds the grandiose spectacle of nature **described by the romantic poets.**

3. A morning chorus of twitterings and chirpings rises from the vast, leafy tree **where numerous families of hungry nestlings dwell.**

4. The author of this book is guilty of using all the hackneyed devices of plot construction and language **mocked by contemporary parodists.**

5. One entire wall is covered by high-fidelity components **from which sounds of extraordinary clarity and purity emanate.**

F. Traduire en faisant l'inversion verbe + sujet dans la proposition relative. Expliquer pourquoi cette inversion est obligatoire.

Modèle: Today's ecologists are **what the romantics used to be.**

- *Les écologistes d'aujourd'hui sont **ce qu'étaient les romantiques.***

  Explication: l'inversion est obligatoire ici pour éviter que le verbe *être* soit en position finale.

---

1. The exercises **practiced by yogis** bring serenity and joy to many.

2. He always votes for the candidates **that the newspaper he reads supports.**

3. Perhaps one day Liza will be the real superstar **that her mother was.**

4. She is impatient to experience the pleasures **that the demi-mondaines who frequented her mother's salon used to talk about.**

5. The airplane **in which the ambassador is traveling** has made a forced landing because of engine trouble.

G. Traduire en faisant l'inversion verbe + sujet dans la question indirecte.

Modèle: History notes **the extent to which the peoples of Indochina suffered** during the war and long afterward.

- *L'histoire note **combien ont souffert les peuples de l'Indochine** pendant la guerre et même*
            adverbe + verbe + sujet
  longtemps après.

---

1. It would be useful to know **when the next stockholders' meeting will take place.**

2. Anthropologists have been unable to determine **how the last survivors of that ancient race died out.**

3. Archaeologists believe that they have discovered **where the legendary city of Troy was located.**

4. I wonder **how much a fifteen-carat ruby would cost.**

5. Does anyone know **the origins of the custom of shaking hands?**

H. Traduire en utilisant l'inversion verbe + sujet après *c'est . . . que.*

Modèle: **The political prisoners escaped** with the help of the jailer.

- *C'est en complicité avec le geôlier **que s'évadèrent les prisonniers politiques.***
  c'est   *que* + verbe   +   sujet

1. It is in engrossing, remunerative work **that a woman's salvation lies.**

2. **Your European guests are arriving next week,** aren't they?

3. It is in Montmartre **that the Sacré-Cœur is located.**

4. **Our neighbors across the street moved away** at the beginning of October.

5. It is on Christmas Day **that the entire family gathers together.**

I. Traduire en faisant l'inversion verbe + sujet dans une phrase introduite par un adverbe (ou un autre complément circonstanciel) de temps ou de lieu.

Modèle: In one of the zoo's buildings **you find only animals** that roam at night.

- *Dans un pavillon du zoo **se trouvent uniquement les animaux** qui rôdent la nuit.*
  complément circonstanciel de lieu + verbe   +   sujet

1. In the middle of June, **the tourist season begins.**

2. From all countries of Europe **flock enthusiasts of swimming, boating, and sailing.**

3. At the intersection of Broadway and West 42nd Street, **a disorderly tangle of stalled cars and trucks were honking.**

4. At this precise moment, **a devilishly ingenious plot is being hatched.**

5. In an unpretentious cottage not far from the railroad tracks, **the blissfully happy young couple set up housekeeping.**

J. Traduire en faisant l'inversion verbe + sujet suivant une conjonction marquant le temps.

Modèle: The celebrity disappeared **as soon as the reporters and photographers arrived.**

- *La célébrité disparut **dès qu'arrivèrent les journalistes et les photographes.***
                        conjonction + verbe + sujet

1. The illustrious actress stood with head bowed **as the enraptured audience cheered.**

2. It would be prudent to evacuate the residents of the area **before the volcano of Mount Saint Helens erupts again.**

3. **When the popular monarch appeared on the balcony,** the enthusiastic crowd burst into song.

4. **After the last leaves of autumn have fallen,** the bare forest begins to compose itself to a long winter sleep.

5. **As soon as the guest of honor entered,** everyone began to applaud.

K. Traduire en faisant l'inversion verbe + sujet dans une comparaison après *comme.*

Modèle: The peasant woman gave shelter to the poor vagrant, **as any good-hearted person would have done.**

- *La paysanne a abrité le pauvre chemineau, **comme l'aurait fait toute personne au grand cœur.***

  comme + verbe + sujet

---

1. He became a millionaire, **as the old clairvoyant had predicted.**

2. He intends to leave his entire estate to his wife and children, **as any good family man would do.**

3. The life of a multimillionaire is far from being a bed of roses, **as most people imagine.**

4. She refused to marry and have a family, **as her parents wished.**

5. I do not believe that the capitalist system is doomed, **as the communists assert.**

L. Traduire en faisant l'inversion verbe + sujet après *tant* + adjectif attribut, ou après un adjectif attribut placé en début de phrase.

Modèle: **The climate is so fine** on this island in the sun that you can take long walks every day.

- *De longues promenades sont possibles tous les jours, **tant est propice le climat** de cette île au soleil.*

  tant + verbe + adjectif attribut + sujet

Modèle: **The crimes** attempted by terrorist gangs **are unmentionable.**

- ***Innommables sont les crimes** tentés par les bandes de terroristes.*

  adjectif attribut + verbe + sujet

---

1. **The nuances** of the human heart **are myriad.**

2. A stranger coming to their village may enjoy, for as long as he pleases, the use of the house and the wife of any adult male, **so hospitable are the natives of this region.**

3. **The joys** of paradise **are indescribable.**

4. Day and night, the scent of roses and jasmine delights the nostrils of all who pass by, **so fragrant is the villa's garden.**

5. **The fragrance from it is so lovely** that many people in the neighborhood go out of their way to pass the garden.

M. Traduire en faisant l'inversion verbe + sujet avec un verbe dénotant une action ou un geste. (Noter l'emploi de ce procédé dans le style officiel et juridique.)

Modèle: Then came a wondrous scene, a magical spectacle.

- *Suivit une scène merveilleuse, un spectacle féerique.*

  $\dfrac{\text{verbe}}{\text{d'action}}$ + sujet

1. **Enter the villain,** a dark, handsome, evil-looking individual with shifty eyes and a sneering smile.

2. **There suddenly appeared** before me **a vision** of celestial loveliness, disarmingly fragile and appealingly sad.

3. **Then the Civil War broke out,** marking the end of an era and of a civilization.

4. **A reception will be held** this evening at the American Embassy for Her Majesty the Queen of England and His Royal Highness the Prince of Wales.

5. **The Prime Minister arrived,** accompanied by the Foreign Secretary and the Chancellor of the Exchequer.

N. Traduire en utilisant l'inversion dans les tournures idiomatiques *puisque . . . il y a* et *si . . . il y a.*

Modèle: The danger, **if (since) there is a danger,** will again delay the ships' departure.

- *Le danger, **si (puisque) danger il y a,** retardera encore le départ des navires.*

  si (puisque) + substantif + *il y a*

1. Her chronic headache, **if headache indeed there be,** prevents her from performing many duties she dislikes.

2. Before moving to a foreign country, they should consider the child, **since there is a child.**

3. I would rather spend eternity in hell, **if hell there be,** than give up the pleasures of earthly life.

4. His father, **if there is a father,** supposedly lives in a city far away from here.

5. In this society we must learn to overcome stress, **since stress exists.**

Exercices de sélection

Pour tous ces exercices, discuter et comparer vos choix.

A. (58) Traduire les phrases suivantes en faisant varier, si possible, la position du substantif objet en caractères gras. Justifier la position choisie.

Modèle: Certain facts we refuse to admit.

- *Nous refusons d'admettre **certains faits.***
- ***Certains faits,** nous refusons de **les** admettre.*

- *Ce ne sont que certains faits que nous refusons d'admettre.*
- *Certains faits sont, à notre avis, inadmissibles.*

Justification: les 2ème et 3ème phrases semblent préférables car elles mettent l'objet en relief, d'abord moyennant l'inversion, ensuite en employant la locution *ce ne sont que*.

---

1. It is **Shostakovich's chamber music** that I admire, rather than his symphonic works.

2. There are **some injustices** that one should never tolerate.

3. One of the guards was bribed to let **the prisoner** escape.

4. The city government has had **many historic buildings** torn down.

5. A crowd of villagers gathered to see **the condemned man** hanged.

6. At the aquarium, children watch **the fish** eating.

7. We heard **a pianist** play a Beethoven sonata with great technical proficiency and very little feeling.

8. The duke gave **his friends diamond and emerald rings that had been in his family for over four hundred years.**

9. This young millionaire owes **his success to his wife.**

10. The author emphasizes the ephemerality and the sadness **of love.**

B. (59) Traduire les phrases suivantes en faisant varier, si possible, la position de l'adverbe ou du complément circonstanciel en caractères gras. Justifier vos choix.

Modèle: **At five o'clock** the marquise, bedecked in jewels, left to join the beautiful people of Paris.

- *À cinq heures, la marquise, couverte de pierreries, sortit rejoindre le beau monde parisien.*
- *La marquise, couverte de pierreries, sortit à cinq heures rejoindre le beau monde parisien.*
- *La marquise, couverte de pierreries, sortit rejoindre le beau monde parisien à cinq heures.*

Justification: la 1ère phrase, dans laquelle le complément circonstanciel *à cinq heures* est placé au début de la phrase, a l'avantage de garder cette courte unité temporelle devant les autres unités, plus longues, de manière et d'action.

---

1. **At midnight, in a corner of the moonlit rose garden,** an attractive young woman, dressed all in white, was waiting for her lover.

2. Be quiet! You have said **enough!**

3. She **suddenly** decided to leave.

4. In order to play **better,** the violinist practiced **a lot.**

5. He has **always** demanded preferential treatment; on the whole, he has been treated **well.**

6. The reporter, **with a cynical laugh,** turned on his heel and strode away.

7. The candidate had the strong support of his party leaders; **however,** he was not elected.

8. She would like to try **everything** at once, but she has not yet succeeded **to any degree.**

9. On the day before the competition, the young pianist ate **little,** though he laughed and joked **a lot, as if nothing were the matter.**

10. The next morning he awoke with a marvelous feeling of confidence and without a trace of his former nervousness. **Moreover,** he was not in the least surprised when he won.

C. (60) Traduire chaque phrase deux fois, si possible, d'abord avec l'inversion verbe + sujet, puis avec l'ordre normal sujet + verbe. Justifier vos choix.

Modèle: This hamlet is renowned for its inn, **haunted by the imperial presence of Napoleon.**

- *Ce hameau est renommé par son auberge* ***que hante l'impériale présence de Napoléon.***
- *Ce hameau est renommé par son auberge* ***que l'impériale présence de Napoléon hante.***

Justification: l'inversion, quoique facultative dans une proposition relative, est préférable ici à l'ordre normal, car le sujet est beaucoup plus long et plus important que le verbe.

Modèle: The attic room **where the anchorite lived** spread forth a diffuse light and the pungent odor of incense.

- *La chambre de grenier* ***qu'habitait l'anachorète*** *répandait une douce lumière et l'odeur âcre d'encens.*

Justification: l'inversion est obligatoire ici pour empêcher les deux verbes *habitait* et *répandait* de se suivre.

---

1. **Let the sky fall!**

2. Perhaps **your employer will agree** to raise your salary.

3. It was entirely without the approval of their families **that the young lovers were married.**

4. I wonder **who my early ancestors were.**

5. She does not realize the affection **that her colleagues and her students bear her.**

6. After many a summer **dies the swan.**

7. **Among those present were** the president of the United States, the secretary of state, and the French ambassador.

8. **The day** of the dreaded ordeal **arrived.**

9. He intends to devote his life to combating the injustices **perpetrated by the society** in which we live.

10. The peasants of this remote village lived simply, tilling the soil **as their parents and grandparents before them had done.**

Exercices de synthèse

A. Sur une feuille séparée, traduire les phrases suivantes en utilisant les techniques suggérées dans le chapitre consacré à l'ordre des mots.

1. After seeing so many things, they had learned little and forgotten everything.
2. In the barnyard you can hear, in the evening, the neighing of the old mare, along with the cackling of the hens.
3. She would stay there for hours, stretched out on a bench, watching the water flow by.
4. I saw you early this morning at your window, hanging some clothes to dry.
5. This cry was answered by another that echoed through the valley.
6. So that he could tell everything, he pretended to hear very badly.
7. Thus the beautiful stranger disappeared; I could hardly believe that we had really seen her.
8. I am indeed proud to present this award to my distinguished colleague, who has worked so hard and accomplished so much.
9. If we catch her at it, she acts as if nothing were the matter, so as to deny everything.
10. I see a little dome-shaped hill crowned by the ruins of an old temple.
11. What became of the leader of the enterprise has never been well explained.
12. I know a trip we can make around here without spending a penny.
13. I almost did not see her at all, yet I surely could not pretend not to see her.
14. At the end of the evening, he was still asking me what my plans were.
15. In regard to him especially, information, questions, and compliments come in every day.
16. Never, never again will the bells of the old abbey resound over the village.
17. He knocked three times, and thereupon he turned and strode out.
18. Her suggestions do not tempt us at all; we might just as well leave at once.
19. These individuals are not concerned in the matter, but later we will need your help.
20. He bent over to pick up the scarf, as any well-bred person would have done.
21. You substituted a longer and much more difficult lesson for that one.
22. The moment for deciding which side she would take had not yet arrived.
23. Perhaps the caretaker will know where the fuse boxes are located.
24. Tomorrow morning, on the Champs Élysées, a parade in commemoration of those who died in the two world wars will take place.
25. All her life she has reasoned too much and loved too little.
26. May all your teeth fall out except one, and may even that one have a cavity!
27. Yesterday a struggling young actress, today a world-famous superstar; such is the unpredictability of fame!
28. Standing at the top of the hill, I could feel the wind caressing my face and my bare legs.
29. It was with serious misgivings that this aviator of fifteen years' experience undertook to fly across the Atlantic in a glider.
30. It is against our principles to impose an unwanted and sometimes frightening freedom on a growing child.

B. Sur une feuille séparée, traduire ce passage en tenant compte autant que possible des techniques étudiées jusqu'à présent.

Wither was not killed in the dining-room. He knew all the possible ways out of the room, and before the coming of the tiger he had slipped away. He understood what was happening, not perfectly, yet better than anyone else. He saw that the Basque interpreter had done the whole thing, and, by that, he knew that powers more than human had come down to destroy Belbury; only one in the saddle of whose soul rode Mercury himself could thus have unmade language. And this told him something worse. It meant that his own dark Masters had been out in their calculations. They had talked of a barrier, had assured him that nothing from outside could pass the Moon's orbit. All their polity was based on the belief that Tellus was blockaded. Therefore he knew that everything was lost.

It is incredible how little this knowledge moved him. It could not, because he had long ceased to believe in knowledge itself. He had passed from Hegel into Hume, thence through Pragmaticism, and thence through Logical Positivism, and out at last into the complete void. The indicative mood now corresponded to no thought that his mind could entertain. Now, even the imminence of his own ruin could not wake him. The last moments before damnation are not always dramatic. Often the man knows that some still possible action of his own will could yet save him. But he cannot make this knowledge real to himself. With eyes wide open, seeing that the endless terror is about to begin and yet (for the moment) unable to feel terrified, he watches, not moving a finger for his own rescue, while the last links with joy and reason are severed, and drowsily sees the trap close upon his soul. So full of sleep are they at the time when they leave the right way.

C. S. Lewis, *That Hideous Strength*
(New York: Macmillan, 1946; Avon Editions, réintitulé *The Tortured Planet*), pp. 228–229.

10 | LA MISE EN RELIEF

Assimilation des structures

61 | MISE EN RELIEF DU SUJET

A. Traduire en situant le sujet en position finale.

Modèle: This new **ruling** astonished the merchants.

- *Il a étonné les marchands, ce nouveau **règlement.***
  pronom   substantif
  sujet   sujet

Modèle: **She** evidently believed in social progress.

- *Elle croyait évidemment au progrès social, **elle.***
  pronom atone   pronom tonique
  sujet   sujet

1. **They** weren't afraid of anything.

2. **These cassettes** are defective.

3. **I** am not altogether convinced.

4. **The cellist** is playing off-key.

5. **This cellar** smells musty.

B. Traduire en situant le sujet en position finale par l'emploi d'une construction au passif.

                     sujet   +   verbe actif
Modèle: **Serious muscle spasms** no longer handicapped the athlete.

- *L'athlète n'était plus handicapé **par de graves spasmes musculaires.***
               verbe passif   agent

1. **A horrendous storm** ravaged the countryside.

2. **The presence of a famous wit** enlivened the party.

3. The use of a good dictionary would improve your work.

4. **A touch of lipstick and mascara** will enhance her good looks dramatically.

5. **The chirping of birds** wakes us every morning.

C. Traduire en situant le sujet en position finale par l'emploi d'une forme verbale impersonnelle.

Modèle: In the midst of all this, **the strangest incident occurred.**

- *Sur ces entrefaites, **il se produisit un incident des plus étranges.***

    il + verbe impersonnel + sujet

---

1. **Curious coincidences** do occasionally happen.

2. It was apparent from their conversation that **they were obsessed with their work.**

3. **To tell the truth at all times and under all circumstances** would be virtually impossible.

4. **Only one faint hope** remained to her.

5. **A great deal of joy** resulted from his generous act.

D. Traduire en situant le sujet en position initiale. Mettre en valeur un substantif sujet par l'emploi d'un pronom tonique qui le suit, un pronom sujet par un pronom tonique que le précède, et une proposition sujet par l'emploi de *ce* ou *cela*.

---

         sujet

Modèle: **The doctor** claimed credit for the recent discovery.

- ***Le médecin, lui,** revendiquait le mérite de la récente découverte.*

    substantif + pronom
    sujet   tonique

---

         sujet

Modèle: **She** repeats herself at every available opportunity.

- ***Elle, elle** se répète à tout bout de champ.*

    pronom + pronom
    tonique   sujet

---

               sujet

Modèle: **Not wanting to communicate with them** is tantamount to refusing their friendship.

- ***Ne pas vouloir communiquer avec eux, cela** équivaut à un refus de leur amitié.*

    proposition sujet   +   cela

---

1. **I** do not believe a word of it!

2. **The young** are seriously concerned with social justice.

3. **To accept a person as he is without seeking to change or to manipulate him** is to bestow upon him the priceless gift of human dignity.

4. **He** was in no way involved in those intrigues.

5. **His niece** knew nothing of his past life.

E. Traduire en mettant le sujet en valeur grâce à une inversion verbe + sujet.

---

sujet + verbe

Modèle: **The long-awaited day** came.

- *Vint **le jour tant attendu.***

verbe + sujet

---

1. In the spring, **the migrant swallow** returns.

2. Many elderly retired people would prefer to continue working and earning money, as **young people** do.

3. As soon as **the guest of honor** arrived, everyone rose and began to applaud.

4. Unfailing is **the kindness** that **her friends** show her.

5. So happy is **the lot** of those favored few on whom **the gods** smile.

62 | MISE EN RELIEF DE L'OBJET DIRECT

A. Traduire en situant l'objet direct en position finale. Mettre l'objet en relief par l'emploi d'un pronom qui le répète et le renforce.

Modèle: After long, arduous months of cold and snow, farmers welcome **the arrival of spring.**

- *Après de longs et pénibles mois de froid et de neige, les fermiers **la** souhaitent, **l'arrivée du printemps.***

substantif   pronom
objet   objet

---

pronom objet

Modèle: It will be a real pleasure to look after **him.**

- *Ce sera un réel plaisir de **le** garder, **lui.***

pronom   pronom
objet   tonique

---

1. We will never see **the good old days** again.

2. They are always pleased to welcome **her.**

3. Have you finished reading **these articles?**

4. I do not understand **this new generation!**

5. Her children? She would never forget **them!**

B. Traduire en situant l'objet direct en position initiale; répéter l'objet sous forme de pronom.

---

objet direct

Modèle: It took six men to subdue **that horse.**

- ● *Ce cheval, il a fallu six hommes pour le maîtriser.*
    substantif   pronom
    objet   objet

---

1. I cannot endure **this heat.**

2. You must follow **these directions** to the letter.

3. Very few people appreciate **atonal music.**

4. He never reads **poetry.**

5. One should never try to catch **butterflies or men;** both give us joy only as long as they are free.

C. Traduire en mettant en valeur le sujet ou l'objet par l'emploi de *c'est . . . qui* ou *c'est . . . que.*

---

sujet

Modèle: **Liberty itself** is at stake in our daily struggle.

- ● *C'est la liberté même qui est l'enjeu de notre lutte quotidienne.*
    c'est + sujet + *qui*

---

objet

Modèle: **It is supposedly miraculous medicine, which** one could take to cure everything instantly.

- ● *Ce seraient des médicaments miraculeux que l'on prend pour tout guérir instantanément.*
    c'est   +   objet   +   *que*

---

1. **Love** makes the world go 'round.

2. **It is power that** men seek.

3. **The industrialists, not the workers,** reap all the profits.

4. **The grace of the ballerina** delighted the audience.

5. **It is her integrity** that I respect.

D. Traduire en mettant en valeur le sujet ou l'objet direct par l'emploi d'une expression prépositive.

---

sujet

Modèle: **Medieval music in Europe** was considerably influenced by the Orient.

- ● *En ce qui concerne la musique médiévale en Europe, elle fut considérablement influencée*
  expression prépositive + sujet   +   pronom
  par l'Orient.

---

1. **The applicant's qualifications** seem altogether satisfactory.

2. No one has the right to criticize **her private life.**

3. He never drinks **sparkling wines.**

4. **The economic condition of the minorities** has improved somewhat, but not nearly enough.

5. I find **his paintings** pretentious and derivative.

E. Traduire en utilisant la répétition pour mettre en valeur le sujet ou l'objet.

Modèle: An eagle, a majestic eagle soared above the prairie.

   ● *Un aigle, un aigle majestueux plana sur la prairie.*

1. All we could see was **fog, dense fog.**

2. **A smile, a radiant smile** suddenly lit up her face.

3. He has nothing to offer but **words, empty words.**

4. **A lark, a merry lark** was singing somewhere in the meadows.

5. The avenue was lined with **cherry trees, flowering cherry trees.**

63 | MISE EN RELIEF DE L'ATTRIBUT

A. Traduire en mettant en valeur l'attribut par l'emploi de *c'est . . . que.*

                                 attribut
Modèle: Summer **is a difficult season** in the tropics.

   ● *C'est une saison difficile que l'été sous les tropiques.*
     c'est + attribut + que

1. Absolute freedom **is a terrifying responsibility.**

2. The Vikings **were fierce Nordic pirates.**

3. The inauguration **will be an impressive ceremony.**

4. The pupils in this class **are lovable little rascals.**

5. Her latest novel **will be a best-seller.**

B. Traduire en mettant en valeur l'attribut grâce à l'emploi de la préposition *pour.*

Modèle: Speaking of books that are hard to read, now there is one that is really hard!

   ● *Pour un livre difficile à aborder, en voilà un qui est difficilement abordable!*
     pour + attribut

1. **Speaking of impossible assignments,** here is one that is truly impossible!

2. **A fine wine!** That's an exquisite wine!

3. **Speaking of handsome men,** now there is one who is a real Adonis!

4. **Idiotic questions?** Here's one!

5. **Speaking of exciting films,** I saw a particularly exciting one today.

64 | MISE EN RELIEF DE L'OBJET INDIRECT INTRODUIT PAR UNE PRÉPOSITION

A. Traduire en situant le complément d'objet introduit par la préposition en position finale et en le faisant précéder du pronom correspondant.

Modèle: One must face **the most onerous responsibilities.**
- *Il faut **y** faire face, **aux responsabilités les plus lourdes.***
  pronom   préposition + complément d'objet indirect

1. It is difficult to resist **the temptations of the flesh.**

2. My friend avoids talking **about her past life.**

3. She stuffs everything but the kitchen sink **into her handbag.**

4. Your paper is full **of spelling and punctuation errors.**

5. He refuses to think seriously **about his future.**

B. Traduire en situant le complément introduit par la préposition en position initiale, et en le répétant sous forme de pronom.

Modèle: The young guest could not get over **their insane proposition.**
- ***(De) leur proposition démentielle,** le jeune invité n'**en** revenait pas.*
  complément d'objet indirect   pronom

1. The witness refused to answer **that leading question.**

2. Each person is responsible **for his own acts.**

3. You may rely completely **upon their honesty and their discretion.**

4. We are shocked **by his outrageous behavior.**

5. He often recalls **his early childhood.**

C. Traduire en employant *c'est . . . que* pour mettre en valeur le complément d'objet introduit par la préposition.

Modèle: Sailors of long ago used to dream **of fabled tropical islands.**

- *C'est à de fabuleuses îles tropicales que* rêvaient les marins d'autrefois.

  c'est + objet indirect + *que*

1. Many professors insist **on publishing as well as teaching.**

2. The students of today show an interest **in the sciences rather than in the humanities.**

3. The head of the company stated his opposition **to labor unions.**

4. This new high-rise building will consist exclusively **of luxury apartments.**

5. I am talking **about her whole career.**

---

65 | MISE EN RELIEF DU COMPLÉMENT CIRCONSTANCIEL (LIEU, TEMPS, MANIÈRE)

A. Traduire en situant le complément circonstanciel en position finale.

Modèle: Piracy thrived, especially **in America.**

- *La piraterie réussit surtout **en Amérique.***

  complément circonstanciel

1. He always craves a snack **at three o'clock in the morning.**

2. The sculptor molded a lump of clay **lovingly and with infinite patience.**

3. The victorious alpinists planted their flag **on the summit of the conquered mountain.**

4. The swimmer felt the water caress her body **softly, sensuously.**

5. He had begun to stay late at the office in order, he said, to avoid traveling **during the rush hour.**

B. Traduire en situant le complément circonstanciel en position initiale.

Modèle: **For three months now,** the lumbermen have been felling trees and sawing them.

- *Depuis trois mois, les bûcherons abattent les arbres et les scient.*

  complément circonstanciel

1. **Slowly, carefully,** she added the finishing touches to her masterpiece.

2. **All along the river,** gaily colored tents had been set up.

3. **For twelve idyllic years** we have lived together, worked together, shared everything.

4. **Very tenderly,** he kissed both her hands, then touched his lips to her forehead.

5. **On a rooftop high above the city,** two young lovers were watching a spectacular sunset.

C. Traduire en employant *c'est . . . que* pour mettre en valeur le complément circonstanciel.

Modèle: Without disturbing the evening peace at all, the birds flew off toward the north.

- *C'est sans troubler la sérénité du soir que* les oiseaux se sont envolés vers le nord.
  c'est + complément circonstanciel + *que*

---

1. **In this very room** Proust wrote the last volumes of his masterpiece.

2. **At seven o'clock precisely,** the entire household sat down to dinner.

3. **With a cynical smirk,** he congratulated her on her success.

4. Napoleon spent the last years of his life **on the island of Saint Helena.**

5. You are mistaken—the meeting is scheduled **for tomorrow, not today.**

D. Traduire en employant la répétition pour mettre en valeur le complément circonstanciel.

Modèle: The detective found the guns **there, right there.**
- *Le détective trouva les fusils **là, juste là.***
  complément circonstanciel

---

1. **Yesterday, only yesterday** (or so it seems), that famous philosopher was a student in my class.

2. I used to sit on the sand **for hours and hours,** hypnotized by the movement of the waves along the coast.

3. **Slowly, very slowly** the bride floated down the aisle on her father's arm.

4. **On this spot, this very spot,** the Versailles treaty was signed.

5. That visiting orator speaks **brilliantly, brilliantly!**

E. Traduire en utilisant *(et) voilà que, (et) ne voilà-t-il pas que** pour mettre en valeur le complément circonstanciel.

Modèle: Surprisingly, a flock of gulls alighted **in the heart of mountain country.**
- *(Et) voilà qu'en plein pays montagneux* se posa une volée de goélands.
  (et) voilà que + complément circonstanciel

---

1. **Suddenly,** dense black clouds appeared **on the western horizon,** blotting out the sun.

2. **Unexpectedly,** a dozen clowns somersaulted **out of that tiny automobile.**

3. **To everyone's surprise,** the actor stopped **in mid-sentence** and ran off the stage.

4. **Mysteriously, in the peaceful village streets,** the sound of a barrel organ shattered the noonday calm.

5. **At that exact moment** all the candles **magically** flickered.

66 | MISE EN RELIEF DE L'ADJECTIF

A. Traduire en situant l'adjectif en position finale.

Modèle: Marie Antoinette's bedroom remains as it was at the time: **impeccably sumptuous.**

- *La chambre à coucher de Marie-Antoinette reste telle qu'elle était à l'époque, **somptueuse et impeccable.***

1. **Breathless,** the exhausted jogger collapsed.

2. Throughout the centuries, the sphinx, **imposing and enigmatic,** stood amid the desert sands.

3. They found the missing child in the basement of an abandoned building, **sound asleep.**

4. The sound of a flute, **high, clear, and indescribably ethereal,** is heard floating from the sands of an Aegean island.

5. The soldiers of the liberation army found a few pitiful survivors lying together in the barracks of the concentration camp, **wasted away almost to skeletons.**

B. Traduire en situant l'adjectif en position initiale.

Modèle: This narrative of the construction of a novel is **remarkable.**

- *Remarquable est ce récit de la construction d'un roman.*

1. The reforms instituted by the new leader were **admirable.**

2. **Many** are the expenses of a couple setting up housekeeping.

3. The powers of the president of the United States are **tremendous.**

4. The bond of marriage is **indissoluble.**

5. The confrontation between the rival beauties was **simply priceless.**

C. Traduire en employant une expression introduite par une préposition pour mettre en valeur l'adjectif.

Modèle: **As for being rich,** Picasso ranks among the richest painters.

- *Pour riche, Picasso compte parmi les peintres les plus riches.*

1. This young man certainly is **ambition personified.**

2. **For sheer obstinacy,** you take the cake!

3. Your friend does seem **absentminded!**

4. Our economy is **doubtless a shaky affair,** more than ever before.

5. **As far as affection is concerned,** she is a little too affectionate, if you ask me!

D. Traduire en employant la répétition pour mettre en valeur l'adjectif.

Modèle: Heads of state should display **really unquestionable** honesty.
- *Les chefs d'état devraient faire preuve d'une probité **indiscutable, mais indiscutable.***

1. He displays a **truly exceptional** talent.

2. The last movement of the sonata has a **uniquely haunting** melody.

3. Wearing a flowing cape of **snowy white** ermine, the princess stepped gracefully into her carriage.

4. These days, children are permitted to watch **horribly gory** crimes being committed on television.

5. I was up all night reading an **absolutely gripping** detective novel.

67 | MISE EN RELIEF DU VERBE

A. Traduire en situant le verbe en position initiale, moyennant une tournure impersonnelle.

Modèle: An explosion **occurred** at the arms factories.
- ***Il s'est produit** une explosion aux usines d'armements.*
tournure impersonnelle

1. A nightmare from my childhood **came to my mind.**

2. A heavy, blinding snow **was falling.**

3. Many options still **remain** to a woman who enters the job market at the age of thirty-five.

4. In France, earning a doctorate frequently **takes** ten or fifteen years.

5. Miracles sometimes **do happen.**

B. Traduire en employant *c'est que* pour mettre en valeur le verbe.

Modèle: **The fact is that** all art forms **perish** for lack of a public that believes in them.

- *C'est que toute forme d'art périt à défaut d'un public qui y croit.*

  c'est   que   +   verbe

1. **In fact,** contemporary society **tends** to idealize doctors.

2. **The fact is that** the Theater of the Absurd **is not concerned** with the psychological analysis of characters.

3. **Indeed,** to Apollinaire, the war **was** a fertile source of new words and images.

4. In the United States, it **is** hard **to tell** the difference between the Republican and Democratic parties.

5. **In fact,** the majority of men still **prefer** the so-called feminine woman: passive, nurturing, and uncompetitive.

C. Traduire en utilisant une tournure introduite par une préposition pour mettre en valeur le verbe.

Modèle: **As an expert on** contemporary history, no one is her equal.

- *Quant à connaître à fond l'histoire contemporaine, elle la connaît mieux que personne.*
  tournure introduite par une préposition

1. **As to cooking,** my husband is a better cook than I.

2. The senator's record is unequaled **when it comes to fighting corruption** in government.

3. **For the writing of fairy tales,** Hans Christian Andersen was a master storyteller.

4. Molière was unrivaled throughout his lifetime **as a satirist of human absurdities.**

5. **With regard to rearing children,** no one is perfect.

D. Traduire en employant la répétition pour mettre en valeur le verbe.

Modèle: The snow is settling and the wind is **blowing, blowing hard** from the north.

- *La neige prend et le vent souffle, souffle ferme du nord.*

1. The rain was **falling, falling continuously** for days on end.

2. The river **keeps flowing** onward toward the sea.

3. Marathon runners **race, race harder** to the finish line.

4. During his busy season he **works, works, works** without pausing to eat or sleep.

5. Day after day, day in day out, my compulsively neat mother kept **cleaning and scrubbing, cleaning and scrubbing.**

68 | MISE EN RELIEF DE L'ÉNONCÉ AFFIRMATIF

A. Traduire en employant une tournure impersonnelle ou un adverbe devant la proposition principale.

Modèle: **It is an established fact that** society unconscionably neglects the aged.

- *Il est avéré que la société néglige déraisonnablement les personnes âgées.*
  tournure impersonnelle

Modèle: The pope will **undoubtedly** make his presence felt in Poland.

- *Assurément que le pape manifestera sa présence en Pologne.*
  adverbe + *que*

---

1. **It is certain that** the reading skills of high school graduates have declined sharply in the past twenty years.

2. Birth control is **of course** gaining increasing acceptance in overpopulated areas.

3. **It is a known fact that** physical exercise is good for your health.

4. **Undeniably,** the national economy has improved during this past year.

5. French cooking and French wines are, **without doubt,** famous for their excellence throughout the world.

B. Traduire en employant *c'est que* ou *le fait est que* au début de la phrase.

Modèle: **In point of fact,** the French are among the most stalwart of races.

- *C'est que le Français est des races les plus vaillantes qui soient.*

---

1. Soap operas are the most popular shows on daytime television.

2. **Indeed,** the prehistoric drawings on the walls of the caves of Dordogne are over twenty thousand years old.

3. The price of gasoline has doubled in the past eighteen months.

4. **The fact of the matter is that** women are no longer willing to accept a subordinate role.

5. Cross-country skiing is an extremely strenuous sport!

C. Traduire en ajoutant un mot ou une expression qui renforce l'idée principale.

Modèle: Every action of hers was **surely** prompted by this passion.

- *Cette passion était **bien** le mobile de tous ses actes.*

Modèle: That man could be elected senator and **even** president.

- *Cet homme pourrait être élu sénateur, **voire** président.*

---

1. You **did** say that your husband was unemployed, didn't you?

2. **It stands to reason that** women no longer think in terms of jobs but of careers.

3. **In reality,** oil is vital to the nation's future stability.

4. **It must be said that** the crisis in the Middle East appears difficult, **perhaps even** impossible to resolve.

5. This is **surely** the first time that his work has been appreciated by critics and public both.

---

69 | LE SUPERLATIF

A. Traduire en employant (*tout*) *ce qu'il y a de plus, on ne peut plus, on n'est pas plus* + adjectif.

Modèle: They claim to be intelligent, but they are **totally illiterate.**
- *Ça prétend être intelligent mais c'est* **on ne peut plus ignare.***

1. His last film was **extraordinarily thrilling.**

2. The final examinations proved **most exhausting.**

3. Simplistic? That is **as simplistic as can be!**

4. My ideal lover must be **infinitely gentle and tender.**

5. When he confessed the truth to her, she showed herself to be **surpassingly understanding and sympathetic.**

B. Traduire en employant un adjectif + *entre tous* (*toutes*) ou un adjectif + *entre les plus* + le même adjectif au pluriel.

Modèle: The reviews in the following morning's newspapers made the director **the happiest man alive.**
- *La critique dans les journaux du lendemain matin a rendu le metteur en scène **heureux entre tous (heureux entre les plus heureux).***

1. She considers herself **the most fortunate of women.**

2. My late husband (God rest his soul!) was **the most generous man on earth.**

3. Although they have been married for more than thirty years, she remains, in his eyes, **the most fascinating woman in the world.**

4. You are without any doubt **the bravest man alive!**

5. He was reputed to be **the most gullible of men.**

C. Traduire en employant un adjectif + *au possible* ou un adjectif superlatif + *du monde* ou *qui soit au monde.*

Modèle: The company's representative **could not have been more scrupulous.**

● *Le représentant de la société **s'est montré scrupuleux au possible.***

Modèle: The cathedral of Chartres is sometimes recognized as **the most magnificent in the world.**

● *La cathédrale de Chartres est parfois reconnue comme **la plus magnifique du monde (qui soit au monde).***

1. The women of Paris are said to be **the best-dressed women in the world.**

2. Their honeymoon **could not have been more idyllic.**

3. In Switzerland we saw **the most spectacular scenery!**

4. Right now my life is **as eventful as it could be.**

5. Some people claim French cooking to be **the best;** Japanese cooking, **the most wholesome;** and Chinese cooking, **the most universally popular.**

D. Traduire en utilisant *des plus* + adjectif au pluriel.

Modèle: The basilica of Fourvière is **eminently vulgar.**

● *La basilique de Fourvière est **des plus vulgaires.***

1. York ham is **among the most famous,** and deservedly so.

2. The Ritz Hotel in Paris is **preeminently elegant.**

3. She married an **outstandingly rich, outstandingly stupid** socialite.

4. Oxford University is **among the most prestigious.**

5. We drove through an **impeccably picturesque** Alpine village.

E. Traduire en employant un adjectif au positif + *s'il en fut (jamais)*, *si jamais il en fut*, ou un adjectif au superlatif + *qui fut jamais, qui jamais fut.*

Modèle: It is a brilliant idea **if ever there was one.**

● *C'est une idée géniale **si jamais il en fut.***

$$\begin{array}{c}\text{adjectif}\\\text{positif}\end{array} + \textit{si jamais il en fut}$$

Modèle: In addition to the richest musical life **that ever there was,** the city is renowned for its theater companies.

● *En plus de la vie musicale la plus riche **qui fut jamais,** la ville est renommée pour ses troupes théâtrales.*

$$\begin{array}{c}\text{adjectif}\\\text{superlatif}\end{array} + \textit{qui fut jamais}$$

1. That is a terrifying film **if ever there was one!**

2. Professor Lenoir, who specialized in eighteenth-century literature, considered Voltaire's *Candide* to be **the wittiest book ever written.**

3. The Grand Canyon is an impressive sight **if there ever was one.**

4. New York is the noisiest city **that ever was.**

5. Albert Schweitzer was a noble, compassionate human being **if ever there was one.**

Exercices de sélection

Pour tous ces exercices, discuter et comparer vos choix.

A. (61, 62) Traduire et mettre en valeur les mots en caractères gras (sujet ou objet direct) en utilisant au moins deux procédés.

---

sujet

Modèle: **This new ruling** astonished the merchants.

- *Il a étonné les marchands, **ce nouveau règlement.***
- *Les marchands ont été étonnés **par ce nouveau règlement.***
- ***Quant à ce nouveau règlement,** il a étonné les marchands.*
- ***C'est ce nouveau règlement qui** a étonné les marchands.*
- ***Ce règlement, ce nouveau règlement** a étonné les marchands.*
- ***Ce nouveau règlement, lui,** a étonné les marchands.*

---

objet direct

Modèle: It will be a real pleasure to look after **him.**

- *Ce sera un réel plaisir de **le** garder, **lui.***
- ***Lui,** ce sera un réel plaisir de **le** garder.*
- ***Quant à lui,** ce sera un réel plaisir de **le** garder.*

---

1. We must fight in order to preserve **our freedom.**

2. **Clowns and magicians** will entertain the children.

3. On the following day, **an unexpected and disquieting event** occurred.

4. **Remaining in self-control** is not always easy.

5. "I wish to perpetuate **these nymphs**," says the faun in Mallarmé's poem.

6. **A stitch in the side and a cramp in the leg** soon disabled the inexperienced tennis player.

7. No one would dare to offend **them.**

8. **He** has not spoken to us for months.

9. The women of today reject **the housewife-and-mother role.**

10. They applauded **the star** for ten minutes without interruption.

B. (63, 64) Traduire et mettre en valeur les mots en caractères gras (attribut ou complément introduit par une préposition) en utilisant au moins deux procédés.

---

attribut

Modèle: Summer is **a difficult season** in the tropics.

- *C'est une saison difficile que l'été sous les tropiques.*
- *L'été sous les tropiques est une saison difficile si jamais il en fut.*
- *L'été sous les tropiques! Pour une saison difficile, en voilà une qui est difficile.*

---

complément introduit par une préposition

Modèle: Visitors are grateful to you for **those unforgettable walks and dinners** in the Beaujolais country.

- *Les visiteurs vous en savent gré de ces inoubliables promenades et dîners en Beaujolais.*
- *(De) ces inoubliables promenades et dîners en Beaujolais, les visiteurs vous en savent gré.*
- *C'est de ces inoubliables promenades et dîners en Beaujolais que les visiteurs vous savent gré.*

---

1. Love is **a form of insanity.**

2. A little learning is **a dangerous thing.**

3. **Speaking of glorious sunsets,** there is one that is really superb!

4. **About small cars**—that one is absolutely minuscule!

5. The romantic adolescent dreamed of **love undying.**

6. He remembers **his trip** to France with nostalgia.

7. They were not thinking of **marriage.**

8. We never talk of **that terrible winter.**

9. The little prince was responsible for **his rose.**

10. One should not obey **an unjust law.**

C. (65, 66) Traduire et mettre en valeur les mots en caractères gras (complément circonstanciel ou adjectif) en utilisant au moins deux procédés.

---

complément circonstanciel de lieu

Modèle: The famous lovers' tryst took place **here on this very spot.**

- *C'est ici précisément qu'a eu lieu le célèbre rendez-vous amoureux.*
- *Ici, précisément ici a eu lieu le célèbre rendez-vous amoureux.*

- *Ici précisément a eu lieu le célèbre rendez-vous amoureux.*
- *Le célèbre rendez-vous amoureux a eu lieu **ici précisément (à cet endroit précis).***

---

adjectif

Modèle: The little boy is **radiant with joy.**

- ***Radieux** est le petit garçon.*
- ***Pour ce qui est d'être radieux,** le petit garçon l'est.*
- *Le petit garçon est **radieux, mais tout à fait radieux.***
- ***Qu'il est radieux,** le petit garçon.*

---

1. **Two months ago,** he suddenly began to take an interest in his studies.

2. **Without betraying the depth of her emotion,** the marchioness bade her lover farewell.

3. **Unexpectedly,** hundreds of bees came swarming **from the gap in the hedge.**

4. **Blessed** are the meek, for they shall inherit the earth.

5. On that night the wind was **blustery** and the rain **torrential.**

6. **After years and years of painstaking research,** the Curies made their momentous discovery.

7. **Defiantly,** the witness refused to appear in court.

8. The renowned poet resided **here in this very neighborhood.**

9. My partner's proposals are **perfectly valid.**

10. The princess remained, as always, **gracious and aloof.**

D. (67, 68, 69) Traduire et mettre en valeur les mots en caractères gras (verbe, énoncé affirmatif, ou adjectif au superlatif) en utilisant au moins deux procédés.

---

verbe

Modèle: An explosion **occurred** at the arms factories.

- ***Il s'est produit** une explosion aux usines d'armements.*
- ***C'est qu'**une explosion **s'est produite** aux usines d'armements.*
- ***Le fait est qu'**une explosion **s'est produite** aux usines d'armements.*
- *Une explosion **s'est produite, en effet,** aux usines d'armements.*
- *Une explosion **s'est bien produite** aux usines d'armements.*

├─────────énoncé affirmatif─────────┤

Modèle: Every action of hers was **surely** prompted by this passion.

- *Cette passion était **bien** le mobile de tous ses actes.*
- ***Assurément que** cette passion était le mobile de tous ses actes.*
- *Cette passion était **effectivement** le mobile de tous ses actes.*
- ***Il faut dire que** cette passion était le mobile de tous ses actes.*
- *Cette passion était **sans contredit** le mobile de tous ses actes.*

---

adjectif au superlatif

Modèle: The reviews in the following morning's newspapers made the director **the happiest man alive.**

- *La critique dans les journaux du lendemain matin a rendu le metteur en scène **heureux entre tous.***
- *La critique dans les journaux du lendemain matin a rendu le metteur en scène **heureux au possible.***
- *La critique dans les journaux du lendemain matin a rendu le metteur en scène **on ne peut plus heureux.***
- *La critique dans les journaux du lendemain matin a rendu le metteur en scène **l'homme le plus heureux qui soit au monde.***
- *La critique dans les journaux du lendemain matin a rendu le metteur en scène **un homme heureux si jamais il en fut.***

---

1. Many useful innovations **have resulted** from that ingenious suggestion.

2. **It is an established fact that** obesity is a serious threat to one's health.

3. My supervisor is **surely the most lovable man in the world.**

4. It is **indeed** difficult to tell the difference between valuable antiques and worthless old junk.

5. The tears **kept pouring** down her cheeks.

6. This is a **mysterious** business **if ever there was one!**

7. **In fact,** the candidate is receiving very little popular support.

8. Their mansion was **preeminently ostentatious.**

9. It is **fully** twenty years since our last meeting.

10. The party **could not have been more amusing.**

Exercices de synthèse

A. Sur une feuille séparée, traduire les phrases suivantes en utilisant les techniques suggérées dans le chapitre consacré à la mise en relief. (Vu la complexité du sujet, il y a deux séries de trente phrases.)

Série 1
1. The little *corporal* showed no fear.
2. Rich *clothing* was placed upon her.
3. *You* have no right to such privileges.
4. A terrible *suspicion* flashed through my mind.
5. I would have recognized *you* anywhere.
6. I know you will like Nicholson's *performance* in *Cyrano de Bergerac.*
7. Then the doctor gave her some *pills* to relieve her suffering.
8. I do not know any more *funny songs.*
9. *A policeman* stopped the woman.

10. That cathedral spire was a *marvel* of stone lacework.
11. I was telling you about the *burglar*.
12. We thought he was a rather *dull lecturer*.
13. I ought to have written to *her*.
14. I have been asleep for *ten minutes*.
15. *Way over there* you can see some smoke.
16. The rain beats upon the panes, *endlessly*.
17. You are getting far *too* thin.
18. *All of a sudden,* she shouted out the window.
19. No one would think of denying that she was *intelligent*.
20. The western sky was *black*.
21. I never thought of selling *this* house.
22. He would like to use his dictionary, but he cannot *find* it.
23. I *heard* it with my own ears.
24. In the distance we could hear the thunder *rumbling*.
25. I did it *just to* show you the danger.
26. She is *undoubtedly* the silliest woman *you could imagine*.
27. *The Star Spangled Banner* is *a stirring song of patriotism and honor*.
28. He faced the examiners *without losing his composure*.
29. April is *the cruelest month*.
30. She does not realize *the advantages* of the situation.

Série 2

1. Of course I have not told her, what do you think!
2. I do wish you would make up your mind!
3. He insists on my being there, and I am quite willing.
4. Tomorrow at five? I will be there for sure.
5. When she talks that way, she is clearly wrong.
6. Where can he be, and what do you suppose he is up to?*
7. It is vital that the very last moments be most striking.
8. Naturally, I do not know; indeed, I have not seen them for weeks.
9. She has not done a single thing all morning; that is downright shameful.
10. You must really love swimming!
11. You cannot make a scene in public!
12. Will you kindly pay attention for a moment?
13. "I watched him quite a while; the fellow is strong." "Sure, I told you so."*
14. What in the world are you scratching around in that pile for?
15. The very first speaker was magnificent. He could not have been better!
16. I did not expect to find her, but I did, in the tiny cabin.
17. Your consideration is really most flattering; please accept my thanks.
18. I would not mind eating a tender slice of steak right now.
19. "Do put on your hat!" "Why, what is the matter with my hair?"
20. Three of them are going for a long walk right now.
21. Tears of pure joy came to her eyes.
22. He did tell us that they would arrive very late.
23. That is an absolutely stunning outfit!*
24. She played the flute with a sweetness that was exquisite.
25. In my wildest dreams I could not have imagined such a thing!
26. He can risk his life if he wants to, but I would not.
27. Weary, weary is the housewife's daily grind; and the worst of it is the boredom, the soul-destroying boredom.
28. You don't mean to say that you let her get away with that!
29. I had never been so downright astonished in my entire life.
30. She went out to work and he did the housework and took care of the children.

B. Sur une feuille séparée, traduire ce passage en tenant compte autant que possible des techniques étudiées jusqu'à présent.

Her topic absorbed her. It suited her perfectly. The woman Marian Evans gave her courage. *She* had not found her love till she was thirty-five, nor her life's work till she was thirty-seven. Jane read her letters, she reread the novels, pored over the "quarry" for *Middlemarch,* lived all day in the social and moral universe of these people. She grew thin on celery and cheese and carrot sticks, and drank six or seven cartons of milk each day from the library's vending machine, to keep herself from overexcitement. For the first time in her life, she was where she wanted to be; she was at one with her task. She *was* her work. Outside, it snowed constantly. One snow followed another. The campus was white and silent. Outside and inside her, all was cold, white, pure. She looked in the mirror of the library's women's room and saw a clear-eyed being with nothing about her wasted, no excess skin or energy which was not in use. Her skin, it seemed to her, glowed with a mental and spiritual electricity, like a saint's skin; she was a person operating from the center of her best will; there were no superfluities.

Gail Godwin, *The Odd Woman*
(Harmondsworth, England: Penguin, The Contemporary American Fiction Series, 1985), p. 214.